C-4087   CAREER EXAMINATION SERIES

This is your
PASSBOOK for...

Transit Supervisor

Test Preparation Study Guide
Questions & Answers

NATIONAL LEARNING CORPORATION®

COPYRIGHT NOTICE

This book is SOLELY intended for, is sold ONLY to, and its use is RESTRICTED to individual, bona fide applicants or candidates who qualify by virtue of having seriously filed applications for appropriate license, certificate, professional and/or promotional advancement, higher school matriculation, scholarship, or other legitimate requirements of education and/or governmental authorities.

This book is NOT intended for use, class instruction, tutoring, training, duplication, copying, reprinting, excerption, or adaptation, etc., by:

1) Other publishers
2) Proprietors and/or Instructors of "Coaching" and/or Preparatory Courses
3) Personnel and/or Training Divisions of commercial, industrial, and governmental organizations
4) Schools, colleges, or universities and/or their departments and staffs, including teachers and other personnel
5) Testing Agencies or Bureaus
6) Study groups which seek by the purchase of a single volume to copy and/or duplicate and/or adapt this material for use by the group as a whole without having purchased individual volumes for each of the members of the group
7) Et al.

Such persons would be in violation of appropriate Federal and State statutes.

PROVISION OF LICENSING AGREEMENTS – Recognized educational, commercial, industrial, and governmental institutions and organizations, and others legitimately engaged in educational pursuits, including training, testing, and measurement activities, may address request for a licensing agreement to the copyright owners, who will determine whether, and under what conditions, including fees and charges, the materials in this book may be used them. In other words, a licensing facility exists for the legitimate use of the material in this book on other than an individual basis. However, it is asseverated and affirmed here that the material in this book CANNOT be used without the receipt of the express permission of such a licensing agreement from the Publishers. Inquiries re licensing should be addressed to the company, attention rights and permissions department.

All rights reserved, including the right of reproduction in whole or in part, in any form or by any means, electronic or mechanical, including photocopying, recording, or by any information storage and retrieval system, without permission in writing from the Publisher.

Copyright © 2024 by
National Learning Corporation

212 Michael Drive, Syosset, NY 11791
(516) 921-8888 • www.passbooks.com
E-mail: info@passbooks.com

PUBLISHED IN THE UNITED STATES OF AMERICA

PASSBOOK® SERIES

THE *PASSBOOK® SERIES* has been created to prepare applicants and candidates for the ultimate academic battlefield – the examination room.

At some time in our lives, each and every one of us may be required to take an examination – for validation, matriculation, admission, qualification, registration, certification, or licensure.

Based on the assumption that every applicant or candidate has met the basic formal educational standards, has taken the required number of courses, and read the necessary texts, the *PASSBOOK® SERIES* furnishes the one special preparation which may assure passing with confidence, instead of failing with insecurity. Examination questions – together with answers – are furnished as the basic vehicle for study so that the mysteries of the examination and its compounding difficulties may be eliminated or diminished by a sure method.

This book is meant to help you pass your examination provided that you qualify and are serious in your objective.

The entire field is reviewed through the huge store of content information which is succinctly presented through a provocative and challenging approach – the question-and-answer method.

A climate of success is established by furnishing the correct answers at the end of each test.

You soon learn to recognize types of questions, forms of questions, and patterns of questioning. You may even begin to anticipate expected outcomes.

You perceive that many questions are repeated or adapted so that you can gain acute insights, which may enable you to score many sure points.

You learn how to confront new questions, or types of questions, and to attack them confidently and work out the correct answers.

You note objectives and emphases, and recognize pitfalls and dangers, so that you may make positive educational adjustments.

Moreover, you are kept fully informed in relation to new concepts, methods, practices, and directions in the field.

You discover that you are actually taking the examination all the time: you are preparing for the examination by "taking" an examination, not by reading extraneous and/or supererogatory textbooks.

In short, this PASSBOOK®, used directedly, should be an important factor in helping you to pass your test.

TRANSIT SUPERVISOR

DUTIES
Under general supervision, the Transit Supervisor performs first-line supervisory duties in a variety of transit service activities. The essential functions of the class may vary depending on assignment and include the following: supervise, direct, review, plan and evaluate the work of subordinate personnel engaged in a variety of transit service activities; schedule and monitor division work activities; coordinate schedule adjustments and operator activities with central control; maintain, analyze, prepare and update transit schedules; ensure proper coverage at the subway stations; use two-way radio systems; instruct operators in safe, efficient vehicle operation and passenger service, including identifying and recommending retraining needs; evaluate problems and recommend and/or take corrective action; prepare and analyze operating reports and records; interact with members of the public and other agency representatives; other related duties as required.

SCOPE OF THE EXAMINATION
The written test will cover knowledge, skills and/or abilities in such areas as:

1. Knowledge of transit lines, schedules and equipment;
2. Knowledge of traffic patterns and impact on transit corridors;
3. Emergency procedures; and
4. Understanding and interpreting written material.

HOW TO TAKE A TEST

I. YOU MUST PASS AN EXAMINATION

A. *WHAT EVERY CANDIDATE SHOULD KNOW*

Examination applicants often ask us for help in preparing for the written test. What can I study in advance? What kinds of questions will be asked? How will the test be given? How will the papers be graded?

As an applicant for a civil service examination, you may be wondering about some of these things. Our purpose here is to suggest effective methods of advance study and to describe civil service examinations.

Your chances for success on this examination can be increased if you know how to prepare. Those "pre-examination jitters" can be reduced if you know what to expect. You can even experience an adventure in good citizenship if you know why civil service exams are given.

B. *WHY ARE CIVIL SERVICE EXAMINATIONS GIVEN?*

Civil service examinations are important to you in two ways. As a citizen, you want public jobs filled by employees who know how to do their work. As a job seeker, you want a fair chance to compete for that job on an equal footing with other candidates. The best-known means of accomplishing this two-fold goal is the competitive examination.

Exams are widely publicized throughout the nation. They may be administered for jobs in federal, state, city, municipal, town or village governments or agencies.

Any citizen may apply, with some limitations, such as the age or residence of applicants. Your experience and education may be reviewed to see whether you meet the requirements for the particular examination. When these requirements exist, they are reasonable and applied consistently to all applicants. Thus, a competitive examination may cause you some uneasiness now, but it is your privilege and safeguard.

C. *HOW ARE CIVIL SERVICE EXAMS DEVELOPED?*

Examinations are carefully written by trained technicians who are specialists in the field known as "psychological measurement," in consultation with recognized authorities in the field of work that the test will cover. These experts recommend the subject matter areas or skills to be tested; only those knowledges or skills important to your success on the job are included. The most reliable books and source materials available are used as references. Together, the experts and technicians judge the difficulty level of the questions.

Test technicians know how to phrase questions so that the problem is clearly stated. Their ethics do not permit "trick" or "catch" questions. Questions may have been tried out on sample groups, or subjected to statistical analysis, to determine their usefulness.

Written tests are often used in combination with performance tests, ratings of training and experience, and oral interviews. All of these measures combine to form the best-known means of finding the right person for the right job.

II. HOW TO PASS THE WRITTEN TEST

A. NATURE OF THE EXAMINATION

To prepare intelligently for civil service examinations, you should know how they differ from school examinations you have taken. In school you were assigned certain definite pages to read or subjects to cover. The examination questions were quite detailed and usually emphasized memory. Civil service exams, on the other hand, try to discover your present ability to perform the duties of a position, plus your potentiality to learn these duties. In other words, a civil service exam attempts to predict how successful you will be. Questions cover such a broad area that they cannot be as minute and detailed as school exam questions.

In the public service similar kinds of work, or positions, are grouped together in one "class." This process is known as *position-classification*. All the positions in a class are paid according to the salary range for that class. One class title covers all of these positions, and they are all tested by the same examination.

B. FOUR BASIC STEPS

1) Study the announcement

How, then, can you know what subjects to study? Our best answer is: "Learn as much as possible about the class of positions for which you've applied." The exam will test the knowledge, skills and abilities needed to do the work.

Your most valuable source of information about the position you want is the official exam announcement. This announcement lists the training and experience qualifications. Check these standards and apply only if you come reasonably close to meeting them.

The brief description of the position in the examination announcement offers some clues to the subjects which will be tested. Think about the job itself. Review the duties in your mind. Can you perform them, or are there some in which you are rusty? Fill in the blank spots in your preparation.

Many jurisdictions preview the written test in the exam announcement by including a section called "Knowledge and Abilities Required," "Scope of the Examination," or some similar heading. Here you will find out specifically what fields will be tested.

2) Review your own background

Once you learn in general what the position is all about, and what you need to know to do the work, ask yourself which subjects you already know fairly well and which need improvement. You may wonder whether to concentrate on improving your strong areas or on building some background in your fields of weakness. When the announcement has specified "some knowledge" or "considerable knowledge," or has used adjectives like "beginning principles of..." or "advanced ... methods," you can get a clue as to the number and difficulty of questions to be asked in any given field. More questions, and hence broader coverage, would be included for those subjects which are more important in the work. Now weigh your strengths and weaknesses against the job requirements and prepare accordingly.

3) Determine the level of the position

Another way to tell how intensively you should prepare is to understand the level of the job for which you are applying. Is it the entering level? In other words, is this the position in which beginners in a field of work are hired? Or is it an intermediate or advanced level? Sometimes this is indicated by such words as "Junior" or "Senior" in the class title. Other jurisdictions use Roman numerals to designate the level – Clerk I, Clerk II, for example. The word "Supervisor" sometimes appears in the title. If the level is not indicated by the title, check the description of duties. Will you be working under very close supervision, or will you have responsibility for independent decisions in this work?

4) Choose appropriate study materials

Now that you know the subjects to be examined and the relative amount of each subject to be covered, you can choose suitable study materials. For beginning level jobs, or even advanced ones, if you have a pronounced weakness in some aspect of your training, read a modern, standard textbook in that field. Be sure it is up to date and has general coverage. Such books are normally available at your library, and the librarian will be glad to help you locate one. For entry-level positions, questions of appropriate difficulty are chosen – neither highly advanced questions, nor those too simple. Such questions require careful thought but not advanced training.

If the position for which you are applying is technical or advanced, you will read more advanced, specialized material. If you are already familiar with the basic principles of your field, elementary textbooks would waste your time. Concentrate on advanced textbooks and technical periodicals. Think through the concepts and review difficult problems in your field.

These are all general sources. You can get more ideas on your own initiative, following these leads. For example, training manuals and publications of the government agency which employs workers in your field can be useful, particularly for technical and professional positions. A letter or visit to the government department involved may result in more specific study suggestions, and certainly will provide you with a more definite idea of the exact nature of the position you are seeking.

III. KINDS OF TESTS

Tests are used for purposes other than measuring knowledge and ability to perform specified duties. For some positions, it is equally important to test ability to make adjustments to new situations or to profit from training. In others, basic mental abilities not dependent on information are essential. Questions which test these things may not appear as pertinent to the duties of the position as those which test for knowledge and information. Yet they are often highly important parts of a fair examination. For very general questions, it is almost impossible to help you direct your study efforts. What we can do is to point out some of the more common of these general abilities needed in public service positions and describe some typical questions.

1) General information

Broad, general information has been found useful for predicting job success in some kinds of work. This is tested in a variety of ways, from vocabulary lists to questions about current events. Basic background in some field of work, such as sociology or economics, may be sampled in a group of questions. Often these are principles which have become familiar to most persons through exposure rather than through formal training. It is difficult to advise you how to study for these questions; being alert to the world around you is our best suggestion.

2) Verbal ability

An example of an ability needed in many positions is verbal or language ability. Verbal ability is, in brief, the ability to use and understand words. Vocabulary and grammar tests are typical measures of this ability. Reading comprehension or paragraph interpretation questions are common in many kinds of civil service tests. You are given a paragraph of written material and asked to find its central meaning.

3) Numerical ability

Number skills can be tested by the familiar arithmetic problem, by checking paired lists of numbers to see which are alike and which are different, or by interpreting charts and graphs. In the latter test, a graph may be printed in the test booklet which you are asked to use as the basis for answering questions.

4) Observation

A popular test for law-enforcement positions is the observation test. A picture is shown to you for several minutes, then taken away. Questions about the picture test your ability to observe both details and larger elements.

5) Following directions

In many positions in the public service, the employee must be able to carry out written instructions dependably and accurately. You may be given a chart with several columns, each column listing a variety of information. The questions require you to carry out directions involving the information given in the chart.

6) Skills and aptitudes

Performance tests effectively measure some manual skills and aptitudes. When the skill is one in which you are trained, such as typing or shorthand, you can practice. These tests are often very much like those given in business school or high school courses. For many of the other skills and aptitudes, however, no short-time preparation can be made. Skills and abilities natural to you or that you have developed throughout your lifetime are being tested.

Many of the general questions just described provide all the data needed to answer the questions and ask you to use your reasoning ability to find the answers. Your best preparation for these tests, as well as for tests of facts and ideas, is to be at your physical and mental best. You, no doubt, have your own methods of getting into an exam-taking mood and keeping "in shape." The next section lists some ideas on this subject.

IV. KINDS OF QUESTIONS

Only rarely is the "essay" question, which you answer in narrative form, used in civil service tests. Civil service tests are usually of the short-answer type. Full instructions for answering these questions will be given to you at the examination. But in case this is your first experience with short-answer questions and separate answer sheets, here is what you need to know:

1) Multiple-choice Questions

Most popular of the short-answer questions is the "multiple choice" or "best answer" question. It can be used, for example, to test for factual knowledge, ability to solve problems or judgment in meeting situations found at work.

A multiple-choice question is normally one of three types—
- It can begin with an incomplete statement followed by several possible endings. You are to find the one ending which *best* completes the statement, although some of the others may not be entirely wrong.
- It can also be a complete statement in the form of a question which is answered by choosing one of the statements listed.

- It can be in the form of a problem – again you select the best answer.

Here is an example of a multiple-choice question with a discussion which should give you some clues as to the method for choosing the right answer:

When an employee has a complaint about his assignment, the action which will *best* help him overcome his difficulty is to
- A. discuss his difficulty with his coworkers
- B. take the problem to the head of the organization
- C. take the problem to the person who gave him the assignment
- D. say nothing to anyone about his complaint

In answering this question, you should study each of the choices to find which is best. Consider choice "A" – Certainly an employee may discuss his complaint with fellow employees, but no change or improvement can result, and the complaint remains unresolved. Choice "B" is a poor choice since the head of the organization probably does not know what assignment you have been given, and taking your problem to him is known as "going over the head" of the supervisor. The supervisor, or person who made the assignment, is the person who can clarify it or correct any injustice. Choice "C" is, therefore, correct. To say nothing, as in choice "D," is unwise. Supervisors have and interest in knowing the problems employees are facing, and the employee is seeking a solution to his problem.

2) True/False Questions

The "true/false" or "right/wrong" form of question is sometimes used. Here a complete statement is given. Your job is to decide whether the statement is right or wrong.

SAMPLE: A roaming cell-phone call to a nearby city costs less than a non-roaming call to a distant city.

This statement is wrong, or false, since roaming calls are more expensive.

This is not a complete list of all possible question forms, although most of the others are variations of these common types. You will always get complete directions for answering questions. Be sure you understand *how* to mark your answers – ask questions until you do.

V. RECORDING YOUR ANSWERS

Computer terminals are used more and more today for many different kinds of exams.

For an examination with very few applicants, you may be told to record your answers in the test booklet itself. Separate answer sheets are much more common. If this separate answer sheet is to be scored by machine – and this is often the case – it is highly important that you mark your answers correctly in order to get credit.

An electronic scoring machine is often used in civil service offices because of the speed with which papers can be scored. Machine-scored answer sheets must be marked with a pencil, which will be given to you. This pencil has a high graphite content which responds to the electronic scoring machine. As a matter of fact, stray dots may register as answers, so do not let your pencil rest on the answer sheet while you are pondering the correct answer. Also, if your pencil lead breaks or is otherwise defective, ask for another.

Since the answer sheet will be dropped in a slot in the scoring machine, be careful not to bend the corners or get the paper crumpled.

The answer sheet normally has five vertical columns of numbers, with 30 numbers to a column. These numbers correspond to the question numbers in your test booklet. After each number, going across the page are four or five pairs of dotted lines. These short dotted lines have small letters or numbers above them. The first two pairs may also have a "T" or "F" above the letters. This indicates that the first two pairs only are to be used if the questions are of the true-false type. If the questions are multiple choice, disregard the "T" and "F" and pay attention only to the small letters or numbers.

Answer your questions in the manner of the sample that follows:

32. The largest city in the United States is
    A. Washington, D.C.
    B. New York City
    C. Chicago
    D. Detroit
    E. San Francisco

1) Choose the answer you think is best. (New York City is the largest, so "B" is correct.)
2) Find the row of dotted lines numbered the same as the question you are answering. (Find row number 32)
3) Find the pair of dotted lines corresponding to the answer. (Find the pair of lines under the mark "B.")
4) Make a solid black mark between the dotted lines.

VI. BEFORE THE TEST

Common sense will help you find procedures to follow to get ready for an examination. Too many of us, however, overlook these sensible measures. Indeed, nervousness and fatigue have been found to be the most serious reasons why applicants fail to do their best on civil service tests. Here is a list of reminders:

- Begin your preparation early – Don't wait until the last minute to go scurrying around for books and materials or to find out what the position is all about.
- Prepare continuously – An hour a night for a week is better than an all-night cram session. This has been definitely established. What is more, a night a week for a month will return better dividends than crowding your study into a shorter period of time.
- Locate the place of the exam – You have been sent a notice telling you when and where to report for the examination. If the location is in a different town or otherwise unfamiliar to you, it would be well to inquire the best route and learn something about the building.
- Relax the night before the test – Allow your mind to rest. Do not study at all that night. Plan some mild recreation or diversion; then go to bed early and get a good night's sleep.
- Get up early enough to make a leisurely trip to the place for the test – This way unforeseen events, traffic snarls, unfamiliar buildings, etc. will not upset you.
- Dress comfortably – A written test is not a fashion show. You will be known by number and not by name, so wear something comfortable.

- Leave excess paraphernalia at home – Shopping bags and odd bundles will get in your way. You need bring only the items mentioned in the official notice you received; usually everything you need is provided. Do not bring reference books to the exam. They will only confuse those last minutes and be taken away from you when in the test room.
- Arrive somewhat ahead of time – If because of transportation schedules you must get there very early, bring a newspaper or magazine to take your mind off yourself while waiting.
- Locate the examination room – When you have found the proper room, you will be directed to the seat or part of the room where you will sit. Sometimes you are given a sheet of instructions to read while you are waiting. Do not fill out any forms until you are told to do so; just read them and be prepared.
- Relax and prepare to listen to the instructions
- If you have any physical problem that may keep you from doing your best, be sure to tell the test administrator. If you are sick or in poor health, you really cannot do your best on the exam. You can come back and take the test some other time.

VII. AT THE TEST

The day of the test is here and you have the test booklet in your hand. The temptation to get going is very strong. Caution! There is more to success than knowing the right answers. You must know how to identify your papers and understand variations in the type of short-answer question used in this particular examination. Follow these suggestions for maximum results from your efforts:

1) Cooperate with the monitor

The test administrator has a duty to create a situation in which you can be as much at ease as possible. He will give instructions, tell you when to begin, check to see that you are marking your answer sheet correctly, and so on. He is not there to guard you, although he will see that your competitors do not take unfair advantage. He wants to help you do your best.

2) Listen to all instructions

Don't jump the gun! Wait until you understand all directions. In most civil service tests you get more time than you need to answer the questions. So don't be in a hurry. Read each word of instructions until you clearly understand the meaning. Study the examples, listen to all announcements and follow directions. Ask questions if you do not understand what to do.

3) Identify your papers

Civil service exams are usually identified by number only. You will be assigned a number; you must not put your name on your test papers. Be sure to copy your number correctly. Since more than one exam may be given, copy your exact examination title.

4) Plan your time

Unless you are told that a test is a "speed" or "rate of work" test, speed itself is usually not important. Time enough to answer all the questions will be provided, but this does not mean that you have all day. An overall time limit has been set. Divide the total time (in minutes) by the number of questions to determine the approximate time you have for each question.

5) Do not linger over difficult questions

If you come across a difficult question, mark it with a paper clip (useful to have along) and come back to it when you have been through the booklet. One caution if you do this – be sure to skip a number on your answer sheet as well. Check often to be sure that you have not lost your place and that you are marking in the row numbered the same as the question you are answering.

6) Read the questions

Be sure you know what the question asks! Many capable people are unsuccessful because they failed to *read* the questions correctly.

7) Answer all questions

Unless you have been instructed that a penalty will be deducted for incorrect answers, it is better to guess than to omit a question.

8) Speed tests

It is often better NOT to guess on speed tests. It has been found that on timed tests people are tempted to spend the last few seconds before time is called in marking answers at random – without even reading them – in the hope of picking up a few extra points. To discourage this practice, the instructions may warn you that your score will be "corrected" for guessing. That is, a penalty will be applied. The incorrect answers will be deducted from the correct ones, or some other penalty formula will be used.

9) Review your answers

If you finish before time is called, go back to the questions you guessed or omitted to give them further thought. Review other answers if you have time.

10) Return your test materials

If you are ready to leave before others have finished or time is called, take ALL your materials to the monitor and leave quietly. Never take any test material with you. The monitor can discover whose papers are not complete, and taking a test booklet may be grounds for disqualification.

VIII. EXAMINATION TECHNIQUES

1) Read the general instructions carefully. These are usually printed on the first page of the exam booklet. As a rule, these instructions refer to the timing of the examination; the fact that you should not start work until the signal and must stop work at a signal, etc. If there are any *special* instructions, such as a choice of questions to be answered, make sure that you note this instruction carefully.

2) When you are ready to start work on the examination, that is as soon as the signal has been given, read the instructions to each question booklet, underline any key words or phrases, such as *least, best, outline, describe* and the like. In this way you will tend to answer as requested rather than discover on reviewing your paper that you *listed without describing*, that you selected the *worst* choice rather than the *best* choice, etc.

3) If the examination is of the objective or multiple-choice type – that is, each question will also give a series of possible answers: A, B, C or D, and you are called upon to select the best answer and write the letter next to that answer on your answer paper – it is advisable to start answering each question in turn. There may be anywhere from 50 to 100 such questions in the three or four hours allotted and you can see how much time would be taken if you read through all the questions before beginning to answer any. Furthermore, if you come across a question or group of questions which you know would be difficult to answer, it would undoubtedly affect your handling of all the other questions.

4) If the examination is of the essay type and contains but a few questions, it is a moot point as to whether you should read all the questions before starting to answer any one. Of course, if you are given a choice – say five out of seven and the like – then it is essential to read all the questions so you can eliminate the two that are most difficult. If, however, you are asked to answer all the questions, there may be danger in trying to answer the easiest one first because you may find that you will spend too much time on it. The best technique is to answer the first question, then proceed to the second, etc.

5) Time your answers. Before the exam begins, write down the time it started, then add the time allowed for the examination and write down the time it must be completed, then divide the time available somewhat as follows:
    - If 3-1/2 hours are allowed, that would be 210 minutes. If you have 80 objective-type questions, that would be an average of 2-1/2 minutes per question. Allow yourself no more than 2 minutes per question, or a total of 160 minutes, which will permit about 50 minutes to review.
    - If for the time allotment of 210 minutes there are 7 essay questions to answer, that would average about 30 minutes a question. Give yourself only 25 minutes per question so that you have about 35 minutes to review.

6) The most important instruction is to *read each question* and make sure you know what is wanted. The second most important instruction is to *time yourself properly* so that you answer every question. The third most important instruction is to *answer every question*. Guess if you have to but include something for each question. Remember that you will receive no credit for a blank and will probably receive some credit if you write something in answer to an essay question. If you guess a letter – say "B" for a multiple-choice question – you may have guessed right. If you leave a blank as an answer to a multiple-choice question, the examiners may respect your feelings but it will not add a point to your score. Some exams may penalize you for wrong answers, so in such cases *only*, you may not want to guess unless you have some basis for your answer.

7) Suggestions
    a. Objective-type questions
        1. Examine the question booklet for proper sequence of pages and questions
        2. Read all instructions carefully
        3. Skip any question which seems too difficult; return to it after all other questions have been answered
        4. Apportion your time properly; do not spend too much time on any single question or group of questions

5. Note and underline key words – *all, most, fewest, least, best, worst, same, opposite,* etc.
6. Pay particular attention to negatives
7. Note unusual option, e.g., unduly long, short, complex, different or similar in content to the body of the question
8. Observe the use of "hedging" words – *probably, may, most likely,* etc.
9. Make sure that your answer is put next to the same number as the question
10. Do not second-guess unless you have good reason to believe the second answer is definitely more correct
11. Cross out original answer if you decide another answer is more accurate; do not erase until you are ready to hand your paper in
12. Answer all questions; guess unless instructed otherwise
13. Leave time for review

  b. Essay questions
1. Read each question carefully
2. Determine exactly what is wanted. Underline key words or phrases.
3. Decide on outline or paragraph answer
4. Include many different points and elements unless asked to develop any one or two points or elements
5. Show impartiality by giving pros and cons unless directed to select one side only
6. Make and write down any assumptions you find necessary to answer the questions
7. Watch your English, grammar, punctuation and choice of words
8. Time your answers; don't crowd material

8) Answering the essay question

Most essay questions can be answered by framing the specific response around several key words or ideas. Here are a few such key words or ideas:

M's: manpower, materials, methods, money, management
P's: purpose, program, policy, plan, procedure, practice, problems, pitfalls, personnel, public relations

  a. Six basic steps in handling problems:
1. Preliminary plan and background development
2. Collect information, data and facts
3. Analyze and interpret information, data and facts
4. Analyze and develop solutions as well as make recommendations
5. Prepare report and sell recommendations
6. Install recommendations and follow up effectiveness

  b. Pitfalls to avoid
1. *Taking things for granted* – A statement of the situation does not necessarily imply that each of the elements is necessarily true; for example, a complaint may be invalid and biased so that all that can be taken for granted is that a complaint has been registered

2. *Considering only one side of a situation* – Wherever possible, indicate several alternatives and then point out the reasons you selected the best one
3. *Failing to indicate follow up* – Whenever your answer indicates action on your part, make certain that you will take proper follow-up action to see how successful your recommendations, procedures or actions turn out to be
4. *Taking too long in answering any single question* – Remember to time your answers properly

IX. AFTER THE TEST

Scoring procedures differ in detail among civil service jurisdictions although the general principles are the same. Whether the papers are hand-scored or graded by machine we have described, they are nearly always graded by number. That is, the person who marks the paper knows only the number – never the name – of the applicant. Not until all the papers have been graded will they be matched with names. If other tests, such as training and experience or oral interview ratings have been given, scores will be combined. Different parts of the examination usually have different weights. For example, the written test might count 60 percent of the final grade, and a rating of training and experience 40 percent. In many jurisdictions, veterans will have a certain number of points added to their grades.

After the final grade has been determined, the names are placed in grade order and an eligible list is established. There are various methods for resolving ties between those who get the same final grade – probably the most common is to place first the name of the person whose application was received first. Job offers are made from the eligible list in the order the names appear on it. You will be notified of your grade and your rank as soon as all these computations have been made. This will be done as rapidly as possible.

People who are found to meet the requirements in the announcement are called "eligibles." Their names are put on a list of eligible candidates. An eligible's chances of getting a job depend on how high he stands on this list and how fast agencies are filling jobs from the list.

When a job is to be filled from a list of eligibles, the agency asks for the names of people on the list of eligibles for that job. When the civil service commission receives this request, it sends to the agency the names of the three people highest on this list. Or, if the job to be filled has specialized requirements, the office sends the agency the names of the top three persons who meet these requirements from the general list.

The appointing officer makes a choice from among the three people whose names were sent to him. If the selected person accepts the appointment, the names of the others are put back on the list to be considered for future openings.

That is the rule in hiring from all kinds of eligible lists, whether they are for typist, carpenter, chemist, or something else. For every vacancy, the appointing officer has his choice of any one of the top three eligibles on the list. This explains why the person whose name is on top of the list sometimes does not get an appointment when some of the persons lower on the list do. If the appointing officer chooses the second or third eligible, the No. 1 eligible does not get a job at once, but stays on the list until he is appointed or the list is terminated.

X. HOW TO PASS THE INTERVIEW TEST

The examination for which you applied requires an oral interview test. You have already taken the written test and you are now being called for the interview test – the final part of the formal examination.

You may think that it is not possible to prepare for an interview test and that there are no procedures to follow during an interview. Our purpose is to point out some things you can do in advance that will help you and some good rules to follow and pitfalls to avoid while you are being interviewed.

What is an interview supposed to test?

The written examination is designed to test the technical knowledge and competence of the candidate; the oral is designed to evaluate intangible qualities, not readily measured otherwise, and to establish a list showing the relative fitness of each candidate – as measured against his competitors – for the position sought. Scoring is not on the basis of "right" and "wrong," but on a sliding scale of values ranging from "not passable" to "outstanding." As a matter of fact, it is possible to achieve a relatively low score without a single "incorrect" answer because of evident weakness in the qualities being measured.

Occasionally, an examination may consist entirely of an oral test – either an individual or a group oral. In such cases, information is sought concerning the technical knowledges and abilities of the candidate, since there has been no written examination for this purpose. More commonly, however, an oral test is used to supplement a written examination.

Who conducts interviews?

The composition of oral boards varies among different jurisdictions. In nearly all, a representative of the personnel department serves as chairman. One of the members of the board may be a representative of the department in which the candidate would work. In some cases, "outside experts" are used, and, frequently, a businessman or some other representative of the general public is asked to serve. Labor and management or other special groups may be represented. The aim is to secure the services of experts in the appropriate field.

However the board is composed, it is a good idea (and not at all improper or unethical) to ascertain in advance of the interview who the members are and what groups they represent. When you are introduced to them, you will have some idea of their backgrounds and interests, and at least you will not stutter and stammer over their names.

What should be done before the interview?

While knowledge about the board members is useful and takes some of the surprise element out of the interview, there is other preparation which is more substantive. It *is* possible to prepare for an oral interview – in several ways:

1) Keep a copy of your application and review it carefully before the interview

This may be the only document before the oral board, and the starting point of the interview. Know what education and experience you have listed there, and the sequence and dates of all of it. Sometimes the board will ask you to review the highlights of your experience for them; you should not have to hem and haw doing it.

2) Study the class specification and the examination announcement

Usually, the oral board has one or both of these to guide them. The qualities, characteristics or knowledges required by the position sought are stated in these documents. They offer valuable clues as to the nature of the oral interview. For example, if the job involves supervisory responsibilities, the announcement will usually indicate that knowledge of modern supervisory methods and the qualifications of the candidate as a supervisor will be tested. If so, you can expect such questions, frequently in the form of a hypothetical situation which you are expected to solve. NEVER go into an oral without knowledge of the duties and responsibilities of the job you seek.

3) Think through each qualification required

Try to visualize the kind of questions you would ask if you were a board member. How well could you answer them? Try especially to appraise your own knowledge and background in each area, *measured against the job sought*, and identify any areas in which you are weak. Be critical and realistic – do not flatter yourself.

4) Do some general reading in areas in which you feel you may be weak

For example, if the job involves supervision and your past experience has NOT, some general reading in supervisory methods and practices, particularly in the field of human relations, might be useful. Do NOT study agency procedures or detailed manuals. The oral board will be testing your understanding and capacity, not your memory.

5) Get a good night's sleep and watch your general health and mental attitude

You will want a clear head at the interview. Take care of a cold or any other minor ailment, and of course, no hangovers.

What should be done on the day of the interview?

Now comes the day of the interview itself. Give yourself plenty of time to get there. Plan to arrive somewhat ahead of the scheduled time, particularly if your appointment is in the fore part of the day. If a previous candidate fails to appear, the board might be ready for you a bit early. By early afternoon an oral board is almost invariably behind schedule if there are many candidates, and you may have to wait. Take along a book or magazine to read, or your application to review, but leave any extraneous material in the waiting room when you go in for your interview. In any event, relax and compose yourself.

The matter of dress is important. The board is forming impressions about you – from your experience, your manners, your attitude, and your appearance. Give your personal appearance careful attention. Dress your best, but not your flashiest. Choose conservative, appropriate clothing, and be sure it is immaculate. This is a business interview, and your appearance should indicate that you regard it as such. Besides, being well groomed and properly dressed will help boost your confidence.

Sooner or later, someone will call your name and escort you into the interview room. *This is it.* From here on you are on your own. It is too late for any more preparation. But remember, you asked for this opportunity to prove your fitness, and you are here because your request was granted.

What happens when you go in?

The usual sequence of events will be as follows: The clerk (who is often the board stenographer) will introduce you to the chairman of the oral board, who will introduce you to the other members of the board. Acknowledge the introductions before you sit down. Do not be surprised if you find a microphone facing you or a stenotypist sitting by. Oral interviews are usually recorded in the event of an appeal or other review.

Usually the chairman of the board will open the interview by reviewing the highlights of your education and work experience from your application – primarily for the benefit of the other members of the board, as well as to get the material into the record. Do not interrupt or comment unless there is an error or significant misinterpretation; if that is the case, do not hesitate. But do not quibble about insignificant matters. Also, he will usually ask you some question about your education, experience or your present job – partly to get you to start talking and to establish the interviewing "rapport." He may start the actual questioning, or turn it over to one of the other members. Frequently, each member undertakes the questioning on a particular area, one in which he is perhaps most competent, so you can expect each member to participate in the examination. Because time is limited, you may also expect some rather abrupt switches in the direction the questioning takes, so do not be upset by it. Normally, a board member will not pursue a single line of questioning unless he discovers a particular strength or weakness.

After each member has participated, the chairman will usually ask whether any member has any further questions, then will ask you if you have anything you wish to add. Unless you are expecting this question, it may floor you. Worse, it may start you off on an extended, extemporaneous speech. The board is not usually seeking more information. The question is principally to offer you a last opportunity to present further qualifications or to indicate that you have nothing to add. So, if you feel that a significant qualification or characteristic has been overlooked, it is proper to point it out in a sentence or so. Do not compliment the board on the thoroughness of their examination – they have been sketchy, and you know it. If you wish, merely say, "No thank you, I have nothing further to add." This is a point where you can "talk yourself out" of a good impression or fail to present an important bit of information. Remember, *you close the interview yourself*.

The chairman will then say, "That is all, Mr. _____, thank you." Do not be startled; the interview is over, and quicker than you think. Thank him, gather your belongings and take your leave. Save your sigh of relief for the other side of the door.

How to put your best foot forward

Throughout this entire process, you may feel that the board individually and collectively is trying to pierce your defenses, seek out your hidden weaknesses and embarrass and confuse you. Actually, this is not true. They are obliged to make an appraisal of your qualifications for the job you are seeking, and they want to see you in your best light. Remember, they must interview all candidates and a non-cooperative candidate may become a failure in spite of their best efforts to bring out his qualifications. Here are 15 suggestions that will help you:

1) Be natural – Keep your attitude confident, not cocky

If you are not confident that you can do the job, do not expect the board to be. Do not apologize for your weaknesses, try to bring out your strong points. The board is interested in a positive, not negative, presentation. Cockiness will antagonize any board member and make him wonder if you are covering up a weakness by a false show of strength.

2) Get comfortable, but don't lounge or sprawl

Sit erectly but not stiffly. A careless posture may lead the board to conclude that you are careless in other things, or at least that you are not impressed by the importance of the occasion. Either conclusion is natural, even if incorrect. Do not fuss with your clothing, a pencil or an ashtray. Your hands may occasionally be useful to emphasize a point; do not let them become a point of distraction.

3) Do not wisecrack or make small talk

This is a serious situation, and your attitude should show that you consider it as such. Further, the time of the board is limited – they do not want to waste it, and neither should you.

4) Do not exaggerate your experience or abilities

In the first place, from information in the application or other interviews and sources, the board may know more about you than you think. Secondly, you probably will not get away with it. An experienced board is rather adept at spotting such a situation, so do not take the chance.

5) If you know a board member, do not make a point of it, yet do not hide it

Certainly you are not fooling him, and probably not the other members of the board. Do not try to take advantage of your acquaintanceship – it will probably do you little good.

6) Do not dominate the interview

Let the board do that. They will give you the clues – do not assume that you have to do all the talking. Realize that the board has a number of questions to ask you, and do not try to take up all the interview time by showing off your extensive knowledge of the answer to the first one.

7) Be attentive

You only have 20 minutes or so, and you should keep your attention at its sharpest throughout. When a member is addressing a problem or question to you, give him your undivided attention. Address your reply principally to him, but do not exclude the other board members.

8) Do not interrupt

A board member may be stating a problem for you to analyze. He will ask you a question when the time comes. Let him state the problem, and wait for the question.

9) Make sure you understand the question

Do not try to answer until you are sure what the question is. If it is not clear, restate it in your own words or ask the board member to clarify it for you. However, do not haggle about minor elements.

10) Reply promptly but not hastily

A common entry on oral board rating sheets is "candidate responded readily," or "candidate hesitated in replies." Respond as promptly and quickly as you can, but do not jump to a hasty, ill-considered answer.

11) Do not be peremptory in your answers

A brief answer is proper – but do not fire your answer back. That is a losing game from your point of view. The board member can probably ask questions much faster than you can answer them.

12) Do not try to create the answer you think the board member wants

He is interested in what kind of mind you have and how it works – not in playing games. Furthermore, he can usually spot this practice and will actually grade you down on it.

13) Do not switch sides in your reply merely to agree with a board member

Frequently, a member will take a contrary position merely to draw you out and to see if you are willing and able to defend your point of view. Do not start a debate, yet do not surrender a good position. If a position is worth taking, it is worth defending.

14) Do not be afraid to admit an error in judgment if you are shown to be wrong

The board knows that you are forced to reply without any opportunity for careful consideration. Your answer may be demonstrably wrong. If so, admit it and get on with the interview.

15) Do not dwell at length on your present job

The opening question may relate to your present assignment. Answer the question but do not go into an extended discussion. You are being examined for a *new* job, not your present one. As a matter of fact, try to phrase ALL your answers in terms of the job for which you are being examined.

Basis of Rating

Probably you will forget most of these "do's" and "don'ts" when you walk into the oral interview room. Even remembering them all will not ensure you a passing grade. Perhaps you did not have the qualifications in the first place. But remembering them will help you to put your best foot forward, without treading on the toes of the board members.

Rumor and popular opinion to the contrary notwithstanding, an oral board wants you to make the best appearance possible. They know you are under pressure – but they also want to see how you respond to it as a guide to what your reaction would be under the pressures of the job you seek. They will be influenced by the degree of poise you display, the personal traits you show and the manner in which you respond.

ABOUT THIS BOOK

This book contains tests divided into Examination Sections. Go through each test, answering every question in the margin. We have also attached a sample answer sheet at the back of the book that can be removed and used. At the end of each test look at the answer key and check your answers. On the ones you got wrong, look at the right answer choice and learn. Do not fill in the answers first. Do not memorize the questions and answers, but understand the answer and principles involved. On your test, the questions will likely be different from the samples. Questions are changed and new ones added. If you understand these past questions you should have success with any changes that arise. Tests may consist of several types of questions. We have additional books on each subject should more study be advisable or necessary for you. Finally, the more you study, the better prepared you will be. This book is intended to be the last thing you study before you walk into the examination room. Prior study of relevant texts is also recommended. NLC publishes some of these in our Fundamental Series. Knowledge and good sense are important factors in passing your exam. Good luck also helps. So now study this Passbook, absorb the material contained within and take that knowledge into the examination. Then do your best to pass that exam.

EXAMINATION SECTION

EXAMINATION SECTION
TEST 1

DIRECTIONS: Each question or incomplete statement is followed by several suggested answers or completions. Select the one that BEST answers the question or completes the statement. *PRINT THE LETTER OF THE CORRECT ANSWER IN THE SPACE AT THE RIGHT.*

1. Train register sheets are prepared at terminals on a 24-hour basis and are used for several purposes. Following are four possible uses of train register sheets which might be correct:
They are used
    I. to maintain accurate and permanent records of train and employee movements
    II. to determine car mileage
    III. as official documents in possible court actions
    IV. as statistical records for future reference Which of the following choices lists all of the above uses that are correct and lists none that is incorrect?

    A. I, II, III
    B. I, II, IV
    C. I, III, IV
    D. I, II, III, IV

1.____

2. The method used to take a work train from in front of an interval and place it behind that interval is called a

    A. cut   B. drop back   C. one ahead   D. relay

2.____

3. When a train is *in the hole,* it means that the

    A. train is in a station pocket
    B. train is at one of its terminal stations
    C. train has been cut out of service
    D. brakes have been applied in emergency

3.____

4. On a train register sheet, a circle drawn around a car number means that the car

    A. is a bad order car
    B. has been cut from the train
    C. is due for an inspection
    D. has been added to the train

4.____

5. The summary of Car trips form is used by the mileage department as a crosscheck of the mileage data cards, and lists all the following information EXCEPT

    A. scheduled number of car trips
    B. actual number of car trips
    C. difference between scheduled and actual number of car trips
    D. car numbers

5.____

6. When recording car numbers on train register sheets, the car number that should be recorded in the first position is the number of the leading _____ motor at _____ terminals.

    A. south; north
    B. north; north
    C. south; both
    D. north; south

6.____

7. Of the following categories of information, the one that is NOT normally recorded on train interval sheets is

   A. leading car number of each train
   B. names and pass numbers of train crews
   C. adjustments to scheduled headways
   D. actual arrival times

8. The type of track that consists of two continuous ribbons of concrete on either side of a concrete trough onto which the running rails are laid, with rubber padding between the concrete and the rails, is type

   A. 1   B. 2   C. 3   D. 8

9. The headway on a certain line is 7 minutes.
   How many additional cars are required to increase the present 6-car service on this line to 8-car service if the running time from terminal to terminal is 1 hour and 5 minutes and the respective relay times are 6 minutes and 11 minutes?

   A. 26   B. 40   C. 42   D. 44

10. The twenty-four hour disposition sheet, which is prepared by terminal supervision, is used PRIMARILY

    A. as a guide for day-to-day operations
    B. to indicate changes due to scheduled inspections, bad order cars, and crippled trains
    C. to designate replacement personnel for absent employees
    D. as a permanent record of special orders and unusual occurrences

11. Following are four statements which might be correct concerning the operation of flexible intervals:
    I. Schedule adjustment by means of flexible intervals must in all cases be initiated and reported to tap points and the command center after no more than two flexed intervals have left the terminal
    II. When the adjusted interval equals the next scheduled interval, the interval not operated must be shown as abandoned
    III. All abandoned intervals must be clearly identified to all gap points, including towers, and must be carried on all train interval sheets and train register sheets
    IV. Any extra trains at the terminal due to earlier schedule adjustments or abandonments must be removed from the station area and laid up until after the period of maximum headway

    Which of the following choices lists all of the above statements that are correct and none that is incorrect?

    A. I, II   B. I, III   C. II, III   D. III, IV

12. Of the following categories of information, the one that is NOT normally recorded on the yard movement sheets is

    A. scheduled arrival and departure times
    B. track numbers involved in each move
    C. disposition of cars in each move
    D. points of origin and destination of all trains entering or leaving the yard

13. A train has been involved in a collision and is now ready to be moved to a yard. However, before this train can be moved to the yard, authorization for the move must be given by which one of the following supervisors on the scene?

    A. Car maintenance supervisor
    B. Motorman instructor
    C. Zone trainmaster
    D. Superintendent, maintenance of way

14. If a train dispatcher notices that a portable fire extinguisher is missing from its location in his assigned area, he should IMMEDIATELY notify the

    A. desk trainmaster
    B. telephone subdivision of the maintenance of way department
    C. signal division of the maintenance of way department
    D. appropriate zone trainmaster

15. When a motorman operates a train from a car other than the front car, communication between the flagman at the front of the train and the motorman must be made by means of

    A. the train buzzer system
    B. sound-powered telephone
    C. hand signals
    D. the train public address system

16. Automatic signals are controlled by the movement of trains across

    A. bootlegs   B. insulated joints
    C. signal bonds   D. negative rail bonds

17. Following are four statements which might be correct concerning car trips report cards:
    I. Buff cards are used for Saturday, Sunday, and holiday schedules
    II. White cards are used when a daily schedule is in operation
    III. Each card represents one train and records the number of trips that the train makes from the home terminal on a single motorman's shift
    IV. A new card is required whenever the length of a train is changed or when a substitute car is placed into the train consist

    Which of the following choices lists all of the above statements that are correct and none that is incorrect?

    A. I, II   B. I, III   C. II, IV   D. III, IV

18. The arrangement of switches which allows the MOST flexibility for train moves from one to the other of two parallel tracks is termed a

    A. turnout
    B. diamond crossover
    C. crossover
    D. turn in

Questions 19-22.

DIRECTIONS: Questions 19 through 20 apply to the type of signal system that is used on the BMT and IND lines and most of the IRT lines.

19. The signal aspect for a *call-on* is

    A. yellow over yellow over yellow
    B. red over red over yellow
    C. yellow over yellow over green
    D. red over red over red

20. The signal aspect which means *proceed on diverging route and be prepared to stop at the next signal* is

    A. yellow over yellow
    B. green over yellow
    C. yellow over green
    D. yellow over red

21. A type of signal which displays either two horizontal lunar white lights or two horizontal red lights is called a _____ signal.

    A. train order
    B. train identity
    C. gap filler
    D. yard indication

22. The signal aspect which permits a slow-speed train movement past the signal into a yard is yellow over

    A. yellow over lunar white
    B. yellow
    C. green over yellow
    D. yellow over yellow

23. Following are four statements concerning repeater signals which might be correct:
    I. A repeater signal is placed on the same side of the track as the controlling signal
    II. A repeater signal is placed on the opposite side of the track from the controlling signal
    III. Some repeater signals have automatic stop arms
    IV. A repeater signal is used to repeat the aspect of the controlling signal for greater range of vision

    Which of the following choices lists all of the above statements that are correct and lists none that are incorrect?

    A. I, III
    B. II, III
    C. II, IV
    D. II, III, IV

24. On the *A* Division, the northbound express track and the southbound express track are numbered, respectively,

    A. 4 and 3
    B. 3 and 4
    C. 2 and 3
    D. 3 and 2

25. A road motorman, paid $20.10 an hour, reports for work on Wednesday at 7:30 A.M. and normally clears at 3:00 P.M. What is his gross pay for the day if he is required to write an unusual occurrence report at the end of this run?

    A. $157.80   B. $160.80   C. $170.85   D. $180.90

25.____

KEY (CORRECT ANSWERS)

1.	B	11.	C
2.	D	12.	A
3.	B	13.	A
4.	C	14.	A
5.	D	15.	B
6.	B	16.	B
7.	B	17.	C
8.	D	18.	B
9.	C	19.	B
10.	A	20.	A

21. A
22. D
23. C
24. D
25. C

TEST 2

DIRECTIONS: Each question or incomplete statement is followed by several suggested answers or completions. Select the one that BEST answers the question or completes the statement. *PRINT THE LETTER OF THE CORRECT ANSWER IN THE SPACE AT THE RIGHT.*

1. A conductor assigned to train service reports to work at 9:30 A.M. on a Friday morning wearing a uniform that is very badly soiled. The conductor's supervisor should not allow him to work, but should send him to the   1.____

    A. uniform distribution room
    B. desk trainmaster
    C. division superintendent's office
    D. chief motorman instructor

2. A motorman of an 8-car train is told that power will be off for at least another 45 minutes while his train is stopped in the *power off* area. The motorman must apply hand brakes on _____ of his train.   2.____

    A. at least 1 car at each end
    B. at least 3 cars
    C. at least 4 cars
    D. all the cars

3. What is the MINIMUM number of lamps required in front of a work area where normal track conditions permit train speeds in excess of 35 miles per hour?   3.____

    A. 4   B. 5   C. 6   D. 7

4. The marking A4 564 on a signal survey plate means *A* tracks, northbound _____ feet from survey number 0 at the south end of the line.   4.____

    A. local, 56,400   B. express, 56,400
    C. local, 5,640   D. express, 5,640

5. Following are four statements which might be correct concerning the movement of trains: 5.____
    I.   A train must not go faster than 10 miles per hour coming into a terminal track ending in a bumper block
    II. A train must not go faster than 35 miles per hour in a river tunnel
    III. A train must never go faster than 10 miles per hour when moving to the left or right over a switch
    IV. A work train must not go faster than 25 miles per hour on curves

    Which of the following choices lists all of the above statements that are correct and none that is incorrect?

    A. I, II   B. I, III   C. I, IV   D. II, III

6. The piece of equipment on a subway car which insulates the contact shoe from the track is called the   6.____

    A. emergency contactor   B. shoe beam
    C. coupler   D. contact shoe slipper

7. A motorman who has stopped his train in a work area receives a *Proceed* signal from a flagman using the wrong color lamp. The PROPER action for the motorman to take is to

    A. proceed with caution and be prepared to stop
    B. proceed at normal speed
    C. contact the command center
    D. question the flagman

8. On trains with *married-pair* cars, the motor-generators are located

    A. on even-numbered cars *only*
    B. on odd-numbered cars *only*
    C. at the middle of each car
    D. under each cab of each car

9. A tower horn signal consisting of one long blast means that

    A. the road car inspector should contact the tower
    B. the signal maintainer should contact the tower
    C. all trains in the interlocking limits must come to an immediate stop
    D. all trains in the interlocking limits can proceed

10. A train horn signal consisting of three short blasts

    A. is an answer to any signal
    B. is sounded when passing caution lights
    C. means that the train needs a road car inspector
    D. means that the train needs a signal maintainer

11. A *12-11* in the transportation department's radio code signal system means a situation involving

    A. a fire
    B. serious vandalism
    C. a derailment
    D. a stalled train

12. A *22-6* in the transportation department's radio code signal system means a situation involving a(n)

    A. flood
    B. armed passenger
    C. passenger under a train
    D. derailment

13. A supervisor makes it a practice to apply fair and firm discipline in all cases of rule infractions, including those of a minor nature.
    This practice should PRIMARILY be considered

    A. *bad,* since applying discipline for minor violations is a waste of time
    B. *good,* because not applying discipline for minor infractions can lead to a more serious erosion of discipline
    C. *bad,* because employees do not like to be disciplined for minor violations of the rules
    D. *good,* because violating any rule can cause a dangerous situation to occur

14. When a motorman stops his train so that the front car is outside the station platform, he may

    A. back up the train, provided the conductor is at the rear of the last car and has positive communication with the motorman
    B. back up the train after notifying the command center
    C. back up the train during non-rush hours if the normal headway is more than 15 minutes and if he has a flagman at the rear of the train
    D. not back up the train

15. A drum switch on a subway car affects the operation of the

    A. side doors   B. air brakes
    C. master controller   D. main car body lights

16. The schedule for a particular route indicates 20 trains per hour between 7 A.M. and 8 M. and it indicates 12 trains per hour between 9 A.M. and 10 A.M.
    The average change in headway between these two time periods is _____ minutes.

    A. 2   B. 3   C. 4   D. 5

17. When a 10-car train is being prepared for service, the time allotted to the motorman to OK the train is generally _____ minutes.

    A. 15   B. 30   C. 45   D. 60

18. During rush hours, when scheduled headways are less than 6 minutes, holding lights may NOT be used for which of the following situations?

    A. When trains are running ahead of schedule
    B. To cover gaps or holes in service
    C. To obtain car numbers
    D. To hold trains when conditions ahead are known to prohibit movement

Questions 19-20.

DIRECTIONS: Questions 19 and 20 apply to the pushbutton type of control panel.

19. When a call-on aspect is displayed on a home signal, the associated signal indication light should be

    A. flashing yellow   B. flashing red
    C. continuous yellow   D. continuous red

20. When a signal indication light is dark, it means that there is _____ route set up and the home signal is _____ .

    A. a; *danger*   B. no; *at danger*
    C. a; *clear*   D. no; *clear*

21. When a switch is in transit, the area of the control panel showing the switch should flash

    A. green   B. white   C. C, yellow   D. red

22. Which of the following statements is TRUE about an 8-car train carrying passengers at a terminal?
    The train

    A. may leave the terminal if the air brakes are cut out on one of its cars, provided it is not the first car or the last car
    B. must not leave the terminal with the air brakes cut out on any one of its cars
    C. must not leave the terminal with the air brakes cut out on a-y one of its cars unless a motorman instructor is also on the train
    D. may leave the terminal provided the brakes are cut out on no more than two of its cars

    22.____

23. If you as a supervisor find it necessary to criticize a subordinate for poor work performance, it is MOST important for you to

    A. be specific about your criticism and not to use generalities
    B. first inform the employee about the mistakes he has made in the past
    C. have witnesses present
    D. keep a record of what you are going to say to the man

    23.____

24. According to Step 1 of the grievance procedure, when an aggrieved employee makes a complaint to his superior, the latter must communicate his decision to the employee within _____ after receiving the complaint.

    A. 24 hours   B. 48 hours   C. 3 days   D. 5 days

    24.____

25. According to the grievance procedure, a Step 4 hearing of an aggrieved employee is conducted by the

    A. chief trainmaster
    B. superintendent of the division
    C. assistant general superintendent
    D. general superintendent

    25.____

KEY (CORRECT ANSWERS)

1. C	11. B	21. D
2. C	12. D	22. B
3. C	13. B	23. A
4. B	14. D	24. B
5. A	15. A	25. D
6. B	16. A	
7. D	17. C	
8. A	18. C	
9. C	19. A	
10. C	20. B	

TEST 3

DIRECTIONS: Each question or incomplete statement is followed by several suggested answers or completions. Select the one that BEST answers the question or completes the statement. *PRINT THE LETTER OF THE CORRECT ANSWER IN THE SPACE AT THE RIGHT.*

1. Following are four statements which might be correct concerning late departures and abandonments due to a flexible interval at terminals:
    I. Gap stations must be notified no later than two minutes after a train leaves
    II. If the lateness is due to a specific problem at the terminal, the command center must be notified
    III. No train may be abandoned to *balance service* when a crew and train are available to make the interval
    IV. When an extra train is run, it does not have to be shown as an extra train when it offsets a previously abandoned interval

    Which of the following choices lists all of the above statements that are correct and none that is incorrect?

    A. I, II   B. I, III   C. II, III   D. III, IV

2. During the rush hours at terminals, trains that are being laid up should be discharged and moved out in a period that should normally not take more than _____ minutes.

    A. 2   B. 4   C. 6   D. 8

3. When a motorman is unable to reach the command center by radio to report a temporary delay in service to his train, he SHOULD

    A. report the details of the delay to a train dispatcher or assistant train dispatcher at the next gap station he reaches and he should also request either of them to telephone the details to the command center for him
    B. contact the command center by telephone at the next gap station that he reaches to report the details of the delay
    C. contact the command center by telephone when he arrives at the terminal to report the details of the delay and he should also report the details to the train dispatcher at the terminal
    D. report the details of the delay to the train dispatcher when he arrives at the terminal and he should also request the dispatcher to telephone the details to the command center for him

4. Following are four statements which might be correct concerning the actions that a towerman must take whenever there is a switch failure and a signal maintainer is summoned:

    The towerman must
    I. establish and maintain contact with the signal maintainer so that all actions are coordinated
    II. be fully aware of the actions taken by the signal maintainer
    III. have a clear understanding with the signal maintainer regarding the position of switches in relation to the interlocking machine
    IV. observe all repairs made by the signal maintainer in the tower

Which of the following choices lists all of the above statements that are correct and none that is incorrect?

A. I, II, III
B. I, II, III, IV
C. I, III, IV
D. II, III, IV

Questions 5-7.

DIRECTIONS: Questions 5 through 7 refer to conventional (lever type) interlocking machines.

5. Traffic levers should be painted

   A. blue   B. green   C. white   D. red

6. When the switch detector light is illuminated, it means that the switch

   A. point is stuck
   B. lever is stuck
   C. is in transit
   D. lever is electrically unlocked for movement

7. The switch in the sketch at the right is set for a northbound move to Track F and Signal 4 has been cleared for this move. To set up a southbound move on Track E, the PROPER sequence of interlocking machine lever movements is
   A. 4, 6, 5
   B. 6, 5, 4
   C. 4, 5, 6
   D. 5, 4, 6

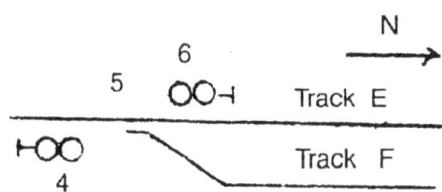

8. Employee assignment sheets are used to designate replacement personnel for absent employees. They are prepared and issued by the

   A. terminal dispatcher
   B. assistant train dispatcher
   C. crew dispatcher's office
   D. command center

9. A light train is a train of revenue cars that

   A. is being moved through a yard
   B. is defective and must be taken out of service
   C. has less than 8 cars
   D. is being operated over main line track without passengers

10. When an emergency alarm box in a subway is operated, an emergency alarm recorder will punch out on paper tape the

    A. emergency alarm box number only
    B. location of the emergency alarm box only
    C. location of the emergency alarm box and those fans and blowers which are activated
    D. emergency alarm box number and those fans and blowers which are activated

Questions 11-15.

DIRECTIONS: Questions 11 through 15 are based on the DAILY TRAIN SCHEDULE shown below. Refer to this schedule when answering these questions. Assume that all operations proceed without delay unless otherwise stated in a question.

DAILY TRAIN SCHEDULE
XX LOCAL

SOUTHBOUND							NORTHBOUND			
Elf St.	Sam St.	John St.	Boy St.	Toy St.			Boy St.	John St.	Sam St.	Elf St.
ARR	LV	LV	LV	LV	ARR	LV	LV	LV	LV	LV
700	712	720	724	730	732	742	744	750	754	802L
710	722	730	734	740	742	752	754	800	804	812
720	732	740	744	750	752	802	804	810	814	822
730	742	750	754	800	802	812	814	820	824	832L
740	752	800	804	810	812	822	824	830	834	842
P	802	810	814	820	822	832	834	840	844	852
P	810	818	822	828	830	840	842	848	852	900
812	818	826	830	836	838	848	850	856	900	908
822	826	834	838	844	846	856	858	904	908	916
P	834	842	846	852	854	904	906	912	916	924
P	840	848	852	858	900	910	912	918	922	930
842	846	854	858	904	906L					

11. The train arriving at Toy St. at 830 is followed by the train which leaves Elf St. at 11.___

    A. 812   B. 818   C. 836   D. 840

12. The TOTAL number of trains stopping at John St. between 752 and 848 is 12.___

    A. 6   B. 7   C. 12   D. 13

13. Between 800 and 838, the TOTAL number of trains placed in service at Elf St. is 13.___

    A. 1   B. 2   C. 3   D. 4

14. The TOTAL number of round trips between Elf St. and Toy St. during the period shown on the schedule is 14.___

    A. 10   B. 11   C. 12   D. 13

15. The MINIMUM headway for trains leaving John St. in the northbound direction for the time period between 754 and 852 is _____ minutes. 15.___

    A. 4   B. 6   C. 8   D. 10

16. An employee loading platform sign is used to designate where a train must stop so that the first door of the first car is abreast of the platform. This sign SHOULD have on it the letter(s) 16.___

    A. E   B. EL   C. ELP   D. P

17. Train dispatchers assigned to locations where emergency equipment is stored are required to check the emergency equipment

    A. twice a day
    B. daily
    C. weekly
    D. monthly

17._____

18. Train dispatchers should submit their bi-weekly time cards to the timekeeping office not later than _____ day(s) after the close of the payroll period.

    A. 1   B. 2   C. 3   D. 4

18._____

19. When a motorman requests a *No Lunch* allowance which cannot be verified by his field supervisor, the matter should be referred for final disposition to the

    A. chief motorman instructor
    B. desk trainmaster
    C. zone trainmaster
    D. division superintendent's office

19._____

20. The emergency team covering under-river tubes during rush hours should consist of a road car inspector

    A. and a zone trainmaster
    B. signal maintainer, and a motorman instructor
    C. and a signal maintainer
    D. and a motorman instructor

20._____

21. When single tracking is operating between two interlock-ings that have traffic control, there is need for

    A. flagging protection only
    B. a pilot only
    C. flagging protection and a pilot
    D. an absolute block

21._____

Questions 22-25.

DIRECTIONS: Questions 22 through 25 are based on the portion of a MOTORMAN'S DAILY WORK PROGRAM shown below. The right-hand portion of the work program showing TIME entries has been omitted, and you will be required to compute certain of these entries in answering the questions.

MOTORMAN'S DAILY WORK PROGRAM
POST ROAD KO LINE

NAME	PASS NO.	RUN NO.	REPORT TIME	REPORT PLACE	PUT ST. LV	SET ST. ARR	SET ST. LV	PUT ST. ARR	PUT ST. LV	SET ST. ARR	SET ST. LV	PUT ST. ARR	PUT ST. LV	RELIEVED TIME	RELIEVED PLACE
TAB	123	104	1259 A.M.	PUT ST.	144 721	222 721	258 750	(404 858	440)	T/C			612	858	PUT ST.
LOD	678	105	129 A.M.	PUT ST.	144	252 736	318 805	(425 912	500)	T/C			627	912	PUT ST.
CAP	841	106	146 A.M.	PUT ST.	201	309 748	338 816	(445 924	520)	T/C			639	924	PUT ST.

22. The scheduled ACTUAL work time for Run No. 104 is

    A. 7 hours, 24 minutes
    B. 7 hours, 44 minutes
    C. 7 hours, 59 minutes
    D. 8 hours

23. The *night differential* for Run No. 104 is

    A. 0
    B. 4 hours, 25 minutes
    C. 5 hours
    D. 5 hours, 1 minute

24. The *boost time* for Run No. 105 is _____ minutes.

    A. 0
    B. 13
    C. 22
    D. 33

25. If CAP, who is assigned Run No. 106, is delayed by traffic conditions so that he clears 22 minutes late on a particular day, the number of minutes for which he will get paid at the rate of time and one-half on this day is _____ minutes.

   A. 0 B. 13 C. 22 D. 33

KEY (CORRECT ANSWERS)

1.	C	11.	B
2.	A	12.	D
3.	C	13.	C
4.	A	14.	B
5.	A	15.	C
6.	D	16.	D
7.	C	17.	B
8.	C	18.	C
9.	D	19.	C
10.	A	20.	D

21. D
22. C
23. C
24. B
25. A

EXAMINATION SECTION
TEST 1

DIRECTIONS: Each question or incomplete statement is followed by several suggested answers or completions. Select the one that BEST answers the question or completes the statement. *PRINT THE LETTER OF THE CORRECT ANSWER IN THE SPACE AT THE RIGHT.*

1. With respect to train connections at express stops during non-rush hours, a train dispatcher MUST hold trains lor meets whenever

    A. the timetable shows an increase in headway
    B. the platforms become unusually crowded
    C. there has been a serious delay and trains are starting to come through
    D. he can do so without causing undue delay

1.____

2. When a conductor reports to the train dispatcher at a terminal that some main lights in certain cars of his train are not lighted, the train dispatcher should

    A. hold that train for shopping and substitute another
    B. order the cars having the defective lights locked, but continue the train in service
    C. report the condition and the car numbers to the desk trainmaster's office and the car inspector
    D. report the condition and the car numbers to the cars and shops department and follow their instructions

2.____

3. If a train dispatcher finds it necessary to pull the emergency alarm because of heavy arcing and smoke beneath a train stopped at his station, the NEXT move he is required by the rules to make is to notify the

    A. transit police department
    B. nearest fire station
    C. trainmaster's office
    D. car maintenance department

3.____

4. A train dispatcher who wishes to flag a motorman past the point at which he is stationed can do so by moving a white lantern in a

    A. horizontal circle   B. vertical circle
    C. horizontal line   D. vertical line

4.____

5. One line of the transit system on which 11-car trains are operated during rush hours is the

    A. Queens-8th Avenue Line of the IND Division
    B. Fourth Avenue (Astoria-95th St.) Line of the BMT Division
    C. Concourse-Coney Island Line of the IND Division
    D. Times Square-Flushing Line of the IRT Division

5.____

6. When the two sets of amber lights which are located above the edge of the platform at each gap station are lighted, they usually signify that the

    A. motorman should release his brakes and start if he has the indication in his cab
    B. conductor should close the doors promptly so the train can start

6.____

C. conductor should keep the doors open until the lights go out
D. motorman should keep his brakes applied until the lights go out

7. With respect to a color-light repeater signal in the subway, it is TRUE that such a signal 7._____

   A. has fewer aspects than the signal it repeats
   B. is located on the left-hand side of the track
   C. cannot be seen until the main signal is reached
   D. is always red until the train reaches it

8. Of the following, the one which is NOT a fixed signal is a 8._____

   A. yellow lantern hung on a column
   B. resume speed sign mounted on the wall
   C. train starting light
   D. station car-stop marker

9. A yellow aspect displayed by an automatic signal means 9._____

   A. proceed prepared to stop within range of vision
   B. proceed with caution prepared to stop at next signal
   C. proceed at 10 M.P.H.
   D. stop and then proceed with caution

10. Because timetables for each station covering the period frorm 10:00 P.M. to 6:00 A.M. 10._____
    have been issued to the public, conductors have been instructed to be especially careful
    in regulating their trains to precisely the prescribed leaving times during this period. A
    conductor can accomplish this regulation by

    A. holding the doors open at each station until the time scheduled to leave
    B. using appropriate bell or buzzer signals to contact the motorman
    C. operating doors promptly to keep station stop time to a minimum
    D. checking his watch against other clocks at every opportunity

11. A recent General Order reads, in part, *IND Division Rail Car #103, temporarily assigned* 11._____
    *to the BMT Division, is equipped with trip on each end of car and may be operated on
    open end of train.*
    This means that Car #103

    A. has a cab from which the motorman can operate the train
    B. should be placed between motor cars so as not to be tripped
    C. can properly be the first car of a train although it is a trailer car
    D. can safely be used as the last car when going against the current of traffic

12. It is sometimes necessary to transfer cars from the Corona Shop located on the IRT Divi- 12._____
    sion Queens Line to the Coney Island Shop of the BMT Division. The name of the station
    near which trains can be transferred from the IRT Division to the BMT Division is

    A. Ditmar's Blvd., Astoria
    B. Queens Plaza
    C. Roosevelt Ave., Jackson Heights
    D. Willet's Point Blvd.

13. Two yellow markers are NOT used on the front end of _____ trains.

    A. extra
    B. collection
    C. work
    D. light

14. A train dispatcher noticed an express train pulling out of the station with a side door open, and he pulled the emergency alarm which happened to be located just outside his office. The train was some distance out of the station by that time, but the train dispatcher could hear that the brake was being applied. He should then have

    A. telephoned the signal maintainer to relay the information about the open door to the train crew
    B. taken his flagging lanterns and proceeded down the track to inform the crew about the open door
    C. telephoned the trainmaster's office to report the incident
    D. telephoned the towerman at the next interlocking plant to place the signals on that track at STOP

15. There is NO rapid transit tunnel under the East River at _____ Street.

    A. 60th   B. 53rd   C. 23rd   D. 14th

16. If the scheduled headway leaving a particular terminal is 5 minutes from 8:00 A.M. to 9:00 A.M., and the 8:25 interval must be removed from service without making a substitution, the BEST adjustment of the adjacent intervals, assuming there is sufficient advance notice, is to dispatch the 8:20 two minutes _____ and the 8:30 two minutes _____ .

    A. late; early
    B. late; late
    C. early; early
    D. early; late

17. The locked *Lost Property* bags which are located at certain designated points on the transit system are picked up by

    A. station supervisors
    B. collecting agents
    C. special inspectors
    D. railroad watchmen

18. An order states that train crews must not be ordered to skip any stops unless *an adjustment of the interval at the next gap point is not possible.* This order clearly applies to

    A. a train which has been delayed
    B. a train which is ahead of schedule
    C. the leader of a train which has been delayed
    D. the follower of a train which is ahead of schedule

19. One line of the transit system which is NOT a four-track line is the _____ Line.

    A. IND-Concourse
    B. IRT-Lexington
    C. BMT-Fourth Avenue (Brooklyn)
    D. IND-Queens

20. A notice reads, in part, *When shop transfers are made up in yards for operation over the main line, there must be enough live motors coupled together to equal at least the number of oars to be pushed or pulled.* Using the symbol M for a motor car and T for a car to be pushed or pulled, a properly made up shop transfer in accordance with the notice would be

    A. T-T-M-M-M-T-T-M
    B. M-T-T-M-M-T-T-M
    C. M-M-M-M-T-T-T-T
    D. T-M-M-T-T-M-M-T

21. An illuminated model board in a conventional signal tower shows the

    A. lengths and destinations of approaching trains
    B. general arrangement of signals and switches in the vicinity
    C. aspects of the controlled signals of the interlocking
    D. routes that have been lined up by the towerman

22. The rapid transit station NEAREST the General Post Office in New York is

    A. 34th Street on the IND 8th Ave. Line
    B. Grand Central on the IRT Lexington Ave. Line
    C. Atlantic Ave. on the BMT Brighton Line
    D. Chambers St. on the BMT Nassau St. Loop

23. During non-rush hours, a train dispatcher at a time point is speaking on the public address system as the doors are opened on a train which has just come to a stop. He need NOT announce the

    A. name of the station
    B. destination of the train
    C. connections that can be made to other lines
    D. destination of the following train

24. Several months ago, the rush hour headway on the Rockaway Line was increased from 16 minutes to 24 minutes. This represents a reduction in train service of APPROXIMATELY

    A. 25%   B. 33%   C. 50%   D. 67%

Questions 25-32.

DIRECTIONS: Questions 25 through 32 refer to the portion of the Record of Traffic Count and the notes given below. Refer to this material when answering these items.

RECORD OF TRAFFIC COUNT

LINE: T2

STATION: CROSSROADS   TRACK: S.B. EXPRESS

Date: April 24

Head Car No.	Time	No. of Pass. in 3rd Car		Total Cars
		Arr.	Lv.	
6410	830	190	120	10
5704	833	190	120	10
6683	836	200	120	10
5996	839	210	130	10
1803	842	210	120	10
499	845	230	120	10
6341	848	230	110	10
887	851	240	100	10
6014	854	250	100	10
512	857	250	80	10

NOTE: 1. Crossroads Station is in midtown, and is a heavily used transfer point.
2. Past traffic counts taken at Crossroads Station show that the distribution of passengers in the various cars of the train is approximately as follows:

POSITION OF CAR IN TRAIN	1	2	3	4	5	6	7	8	9	10
Arriving car load in percent of most heavily loaded arriving car	60	80	100	100	100	100	90	90	80	70
Leaving car load in percent of most heavily loaded leaving car	70	100	100	80	60	50	80	100	100	100

25. The number of passengers in the first car of the first train shown in the tabulation when it arrived in Crossroads Station was about

    A. 133   B. 126   C. 114   D. 108

26. The number of passengers in the last car of the 851 interval when it left Crossroads Station was about

    A. 190   B. 120   C. 100   D. 80

27. The total number of passengers on all ten cars of the 836 interval when it arrived at Crossroads Station was about

    A. 2000   B. 1740   C. 1620   D. 1400

28. The total number of passengers on all ten cars of the 830 interval when it left Crossroads Station was about

    A. 1400   B. 1080   C. 1044   D. 1008

29. Considering that Crossroads Station is a heavily used transfer point, the total number of passengers alighting from the 3rd cars of all of the ten trains shown MOST probably was

   A. 980
   B. between 980 and 1080
   C. 1080
   D. more than 1080

30. The total number of passengers by which the arriving load on all ten cars of the 845 interval exceeded the leaving load on that interval was

   A. 2001   B. 1080   C. 1008   D. 993

31. Of the following conclusions that may be drawn from examination of the car numbers in the first column, the one MOST likely to be correct is that

   A. at least 6000 cars are assigned to this service
   B. alternate trains have different destinations
   C. any car can be coupled in a train with any other car
   D. more than one type of car equipment is in use

32. From examination of the number of passengers arriving and leaving on successive trains, it is PROBABLY valid to conclude that

   A. many of the passengers exiting at Crossroads Station must report to work by 9:00 A.M.
   B. most people using line T2 southbound get off at or before Crossroads Station
   C. people riding past Crossroads Station generally report to work later than 9:00 A.M.
   D. line T2 is operating at practically its maximum capacity

33. With respect to entering upon and crossing the tracks in the subway, it is PROBABLY correct to say of a train dispatcher stationed at an intermediate time-point that such action is

   A. inexcusable at any time
   B. likely to be required very seldom
   C. probably required whenever there is a train delay
   D. probably required whenever it is necessary to transmit messages to train crews

34. When a N.Y.C.T.A. first aid kit is opened, it is NOT necessary to report the

   A. name of the person for whom the kit was opened
   B. kind of injury involved
   C. amount of each material used
   D. last previous date on which the kit was opened

35. An *0* displayed on the heat and ventilation board at a terminal during the winter season is an indication to crews that NO

   A. heat is to be turned on
   B. change is to be made in heating or ventilation
   C. windows are to be opened
   D. ventilators are to be closed

36. A ten-car train took 6 minutes to travel between two stations which are 3 miles apart. The average speed of the train was _____ M.P.H.

   A. 20   B. 25   C. 30   D. 35

37. The latest cars on the transit system are equipped with roller bearings which allow these cars to roll more easily than cars not so equipped. From the standpoint of operating personnel, the MOST important of the following consequences of rolling more easily is that the

    A. new trains are less noisy when rounding curves
    B. train crews must be alert to prevent rolling at certain station stops
    C. new trains can reach much higher speeds than older trains
    D. train crews are relieved of having to report hot bearings

37.____

38. In certain cases of single-track operation, a motorman is designated as *pilot* and no train may be admitted to the single-track without this designated *pilot* on board. Under this arrangement, it is clear that

    A. short trains must be run to avoid fatiguing the *pilot*
    B. flagmen are not needed
    C. regular train schedules are necessarily maintained without change
    D. two trains will not ordinarily follow one another in the same direction

38.____

39. The one of the following which is a train speed restriction in full accord with the rules and regulations is that a train is restricted to a maximum speed of

    A. 35 M.P.H. when skipping a station
    B. 25 M.P.H. when in an under-river tube
    C. 15 M.P.H. when entering a terminal
    D. 10 M.P.H. when not carrying passengers

39.____

40. A recent order requires that when motormen are operating trains in yards or other restricted areas they must operate from a standing position in the cab. The MOST probable reason for this requirement is that the standing position makes it easier for the motorman to

    A. read hand signals from the tower
    B. manipulate the train controls
    C. read dwarf signal indications
    D. see persons close to the trainway

40.____

41. The order in which employees in a particular title are scheduled to make their picks of tours of duty is determined PRIMARILY by each employee's

    A. last name, the names being arranged in alphabetical order
    B. length of service in the particular title
    C. attendance and service rating credit
    D. total length of service in the transit system

41.____

42. If a train dispatcher hears a long-short-long-short whistle signal from a train which is entering the station, the BEST of the following moves for him to make is to

    A. notify the signal maintainer
    B. send a platformman to see the motorman
    C. notify the trainmaster
    D. pull the emergency alarm

42.____

43. One entry that a train dispatcher is NOT required to make on a train register sheet is the

    A. name of the dispatcher
    B. reason for a late arrival
    C. name of the yard motorman on a put-in train
    D. name of the conductor on a regular passenger train

44. Certain lost articles turned in at terminals are required to be forwarded to the office by special messenger as soon as possible after being turned in. One such lost article would be a

    A. wallet containing considerable money
    B. loaded pistol
    C. hamper of fish
    D. press-type camera loaded with film

45. When a call-on signal in the subway is illuminated, the colors displayed on the home signal above the call-on are

    A. green over red   B. yellow over yellow
    C. red over yellow   D. red over red

46. An A.V.A. day may be accumulated by an hourly-rated employee as a consequence of being required to work

    A. four hours immediately following his regular tour
    B. on both Saturday and Sunday of the same weekend
    C. on a paid holiday
    D. on his regular day off

47. Because of changes in car construction, 9-car trains of the newest type are being operated on certain lines of the IRT Division where 10-car trains of the older type are still in operation. By logical reasoning, the change that is MOST probably the cause of running the shorter trains of new cars is the

    A. use of fluorescent instead of incandescent lighting
    B. addition of destination signs on the front and rear
    C. rearrangement of the side doors
    D. introduction of higher accelerating and braking rates

48. In addition to having supervision over assistant train dispatchers, the train dispatcher at a terminal has supervision over

    A. yard motormen, conductors, and car maintainers
    B. platformmen, assistant motorman instructions, and signal maintainers
    C. conductors in train service, platformmen, and road motormen
    D. road motormen, yard motormen, and signal maintainers

49. If a train that is carrying considerably less than a normal load is followed by one carrying considerably more than a normal load for the time of day and line involved, it is MOST likely that

    A. the first train is ahead of schedule and the second is on time
    B. the first train is on time and the second is behind schedule

C. both trains are ahead of schedule
D. both trains are behind schedule

50. When necessary to give a hand signal permitting a train to pass an interlocking signal indicating STOP, such hand signal must NOT be given until the 50.____

   A. trainmaster has given his O.K.
   B. train has come to a stop
   C. motorman blows two blasts of the train whistle
   D. train ahead has cleared the interlocking

KEY (CORRECT ANSWERS)

1. D	11. C	21. B	31. D	41. B
2. C	12. B	22. A	32. A	42. B
3. C	13. A	23. D	33. B	43. A
4. D	14. C	24. B	34. D	44. A
5. A	15. C	25. C	35. A	45. D
6. C	16. A	26. C	36. C	46. C
7. B	17. B	27. B	37. B	47. C
8. A	18. A	28. D	38. D	48. C
9. B	19. A	29. D	39. C	49. A
10. A	20. C	30. D	40. D	50. B

TEST 2

DIRECTIONS: Each question or incomplete statement is followed by several suggested answers or completions. Select the one that BEST answers the question or completes the statement. *PRINT THE LETTER OF THE CORRECT ANSWER IN THE SPACE AT THE RIGHT.*

1. The GREATEST number of passengers would probably be inconvenienced if, as a result of having the wrong marker lights displayed on the front end of a train,

    A. some passengers boarded the wrong train
    B. a towerman lined up and the motorman accepted the wrong route
    C. a platformman announced the wrong destination
    D. a flagman held up the train unnecessarily

2. Assume that you are a witness to an accident in the subway and that a stranger starts to question you about it.
   According to the rules, your proper action is to

    A. ask him for his credentials
    B. refer him to the transit authority legal department
    C. answer only those questions about which you have firsthand information
    D. telephone the trainmaster's office and request instructions

3. An assistant train dispatcher suspects that the man who is to relieve him is under the influence of liquor. In this case, the assistant dispatcher should

    A. refuse relief and continue on duty without taking any other action
    B. accept relief and ignore the situation, since it is no longer his responsibility
    C. accept relief but stay around awhile to see if the reliever can work properly
    D. refuse relief and report his suspicion to the dispatcher or trainmaster

4. At a subway station located in the financial district of Manhattan, an assistant train dispatcher could normally expect the GREATEST concentration of passenger traffic to occur during the weekday hour between

    A. 4:30 P.M. and 5:30 P.M.
    B. 5:30 P.M. and 6:30 P.M.
    C. 7:00 A.M. and 8:00 A.M.
    D. 9:00 A.M. and 10:00 A.M.

5. A subway passenger CANNOT go directly (without changing trains) from

    A. Manhattan to Brooklyn
    B. Queens to Brooklyn
    C. Queens to The Bronx
    D. Brooklyn to The Bronx

6. A rule of the subway system is that the transit police department MUST be notified first whenever an ambulance is needed. A logical reason for this rule is to

    A. help in apprehending legal offenders
    B. enable the transit police to check the need for an ambulance
    C. prevent duplication of calls
    D. prevent unnecessary ambulance calls

7. When an unusual situation arises, and you cannot contact your immediate supervisor to check the method of handling the situation, it would be BEST for you to

A. ask some of the experienced motormen at your terminal for their advice
B. telephone to another assistant dispatcher for advice
C. telephone the trainmaster's office for instructions
D. take no action until your superior returns

Questions 8-16.

DIRECTIONS: Questions 8 through 16 are based on the paragraph below. Refer to this paragraph when answering these questions.

At about 3 o'clock on a weekday afternoon, a southbound passenger express train came to a stop at a red automatic signal midway between stations. After about three minutes, conductor Johnson came forward and asked motorman Smith why the train was stopped and how long it would stay, because it was his (the conductor's) duty according to rules to notify the passengers. Smith did not know the reason and together with Johnson decided to call up the trainmaster's office to find out the facts. They walked to the nearest blue light, Smith taking his reverser key and brake handle with him. When they reached the blue light location, Smith pulled the operating handle of the emergency alarm box to remove power from the third rail as insurance that no unauthorized person could start the train in his absence; Johnson then used the telephone to call the trainmaster's office. Johnson found out that the train ahead had a grounded master controller in the operating can and that as soon as power was restored to the third rail Smith would have to pull up to the train ahead and transfer its passengers to his train. This was done, and the disabled train was ordered out of service while Johnson's train continued in regular passenger service. The delay to Johnson's train at the scene was 15 minutes. After they arrived at their home terminal (the north terminal of the line), Smith and Johnson made written reports of the incident.

8. The MOST serious error or infraction of the rules committed by Johnson was   8._____

    A. leaving the train unattended
    B. failing to wait four minutes before going forward
    C. not notifying the passengers
    D. waiting as long as three minutes before going forward

9. One of Smith's actions which was ENTIRELY correct was   9._____

    A. pulling the emergency alarm
    B. having Johnson accompany him
    C. taking the reverser key and brake handle along when he got off the train
    D. leaving his train at the signal instead of pulling up to the blue light

10. In making out written reports when they reached their home terminal, Smith and Johnson   10._____

    A. acted in accordance with the rules and regulations of the N.Y.C.T.A.
    B. did unnecessary extra work because they had already reported the incident to the trainmaster by telephone
    C. waited too long; they should have made written reports at the first gap station
    D. went beyond the rules; the delay was only 15 minutes which does not require any reports

11. The trainmaster overlooked the opportunity to stress a safety precaution in that he 11.____

    A. allowed Smith's train to pull up to the train ahead
    B. permitted the passengers to walk from the disabled train to the following one
    C. had the train with the grounded master controller taken out of service
    D. failed to remind Johnson to open the conductor's valve on the train ahead while the passengers were transferring

12. In order for Smith to be able to pass the red signal and close in on the train ahead, he MUST have first 12.____

    A. telephoned the nearby tower and had the towerman clear the signal
    B. whistled for the signal maintainer to tie down the automatic stop
    C. keyed-by the signal as prescribed in the book of rules
    D. telephoned the section dispatcher to send a flagman to flag him by

13. Before leaving his train to make the telephone call, the motorman should have 13.____

    A. sounded the appropriate whistle signal
    B. set up one or more hand brakes
    C. opened the conductor's valve on the head end
    D. cut in the car emergency lights

14. Pulling of the emergency alarm by Smith showed 14.____

    A. quick thinking; he probably saved the train ahead from further damage
    B. lack of thought; there was no trouble in his area to warrant such action
    C. knowledge of the rules; such action is required in similar situations
    D. consideration for passenger safety; this action probably avoided panic

15. The aspect of the signal at which Smith stopped his train was PROBABLY 15.____

    A. two red lights above a yellow light
    B. two red lights, one above the other
    C. a single red light
    D. two red lights, side by side

16. The amount of delay to Smith and Johnson in returning to their home terminal 16.____

    A. must have been exactly 15 minutes
    B. depended mainly on the scheduled running time between terminals
    C. may have been more or less than 15 minutes
    D. depended on how quickly a replacement for the train taken out of service was obtained

17. One positive way in which a single-light interlocking color-light signal can be distinguished from an automatic color-light signal is by observing the 17.____

    A. differences in colors displayed
    B. inscription on the number plate
    C. shape of the lenses
    D. signal mounting

18. As part of his regular duties, an assistant train dispatcher may be required to   18.____

    A. instruct newly appointed towermen in his section
    B. keep a gap sheet at a specified location
    C. make certain tests of trains at his terminal
    D. take charge of a yard

19. If an assistant train dispatcher located in an interlocking tower wants to contact the signal   19.____
    maintainer, the tower horn signal to be sounded is _____ blast(s).

    A. two long and one short   B. one long and one short
    C. three short   D. two short and one long

20. The terminal which is NOT elevated is _____ Line.   20.____

    A. Far Rockaway on the Rockaway
    B. Stillwell Avenue on the Coney Island
    C. Van Cortlandt Park on the Broadway-7th Avenue
    D. 207th Street on the Washington Heights

21. If an emergency alarm box located on a four-track section of the subway is pulled, it will   21.____
    cause third rail power to be removed from

    A. the one track nearest the box only
    B. both local tracks only
    C. both express tracks only
    D. all four tracks

22. The gauge of rail is the distance between the   22.____

    A. inside edges of the running rails
    B. outside edges of the running rails
    C. centers of the third rail and the near running rail
    D. centers of the third rail and the far running rail

23. The service on a certain four-track line consists of 20 trains per hour on each express   23.____
    track and 16 trains per hour on each local track. The total number of all trains passing a
    given point on this line in any 10-minute period is

    A. 6   B. 9   C. 12   D. 15

24. If the distance between two signals on the transit system is 750 feet and one signal is at   24.____
    stationing 1275 + 20, the other could be stationing

    A. 525 + 20   B. 1200 + 70   C. 1282 + 70   D. 2025 + 20

25. If a passenger train arrives at a time point ahead of time, the assistant train dispatcher   25.____
    could expect to find this train's

    A. follower heavily loaded   B. follower lightly loaded
    C. leader heavily loaded   D. leader lightly loaded

26. On a run between two express stops, an express train passes four local stations. If the average time required for a local train to brake, make a station stop, and accelerate back to normal speed is 45 seconds for each station, then the time that can be saved by going express rather than local between these two express stops is NEAREST to _____ minute(s).

 A. one B. two C. three D. four

Questions 27-41.

DIRECTIONS: Questions 27 through 41 are based on the station layout and portion of a gap sheet for station C shown below and on the following page. Refer to this material when answering these questions. Station C is a time point on the Lake Line, which has no branch lines. Operations proceed without delays unless otherwise stated in a question.

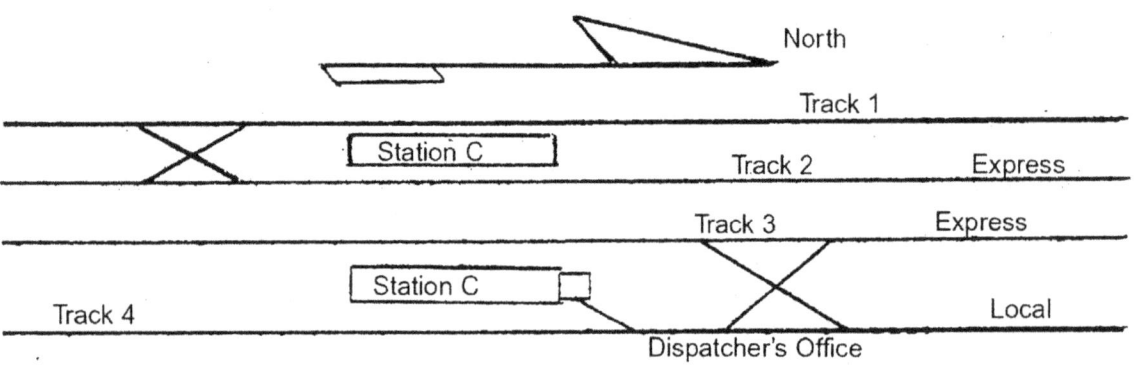

GAP SHEET - STATION C - DAILY

| \multicolumn{3}{c}{SOUTHBOUND} | \multicolumn{3}{c}{NORTHBOUND} |

SOUTHBOUND			NORTHBOUND		
RUN NO.	LV LOCAL	LV EXPRESS	RUN NO.	LV LOCAL	LV EXPRESS
10	1010		11	1011	
12		1010	13		1012
14	1015		15	1017	
16		1016	17		1018
18	1020		19	1023	
20		1022	21		1024
22	1026		23	1030	
24		1028	25		1032
26	1032		27	1040	
28		1034	29		1040
11	1040		10	1050	
32		1040	31		1050
19	1050		18	1100	
34		1050	33		1100
23	1100		26	1112	
13		1100	12		1112
27	1110		11	1124	
21		1110	20		1124
10	1120		19	1136	
25		1120	28		1136
18	1130		22	1148	
29		1130	32		1148
31		1140	10	1200	
15	1142		24		1200
33		1150	18	1212	
11	1154		21		1212
12		1202	15	1224	
19	1206		25		1224
20		1214	11	1236	
22	1218	1226	29		1236
28			19	1248	
10	1230		31		1248
32		1238	22	100	
18	1242		33		100
24		1250	10	110	
15	1254		12		112
21		102	18	120	
11	106		20		124
25		114	35	130	
19	116		28		136
29		126	15	140	
36	126		32		146
			11	150	
			24		156

27. One crew which evidently clears after arrival at the south local terminal is the crew on run number   27._____

    A. 10   B. 14   C. 18   D. 22

28. One crew which evidently clears after arrival at the north express terminal is the crew on run number   28._____

    A. 13   B. 17   C. 21   D. 25

29. Assuming that crews are allowed five minutes between arrival and leaving at each terminal, the terminal-to-terminal running time for express run number 29 on the trip leaving station C at 1040 is   29._____

    A. 1 hr. 56 min.   B. 1 hr. 46 min.
    C. 58 min.   D. 53 min.

30. The scheduled round trip time for local run number 10 leaving station C northbound at 1050 is _____ minutes.   30._____

    A. 70   B. 60   C. 50   D. 40

31. Assuming a five minute relay at the terminal, the running time from station C to the north terminal for run number 18 on the trip leaving station C at 1100 is _____ minutes.   31._____

    A. 12 1/2   B. 15   C. 25   D. 30

32. Run numbers 13 and 23 southbound are *meets* at 1100. If run number 23 is one minute late, the proper action to take is to   32._____

    A. hold run numbers 13 and 21 one-half minute each
    B. let the express leave on time without a meet
    C. hold run number 13 for one minute
    D. hole run number 21 for the meet

33. If run number 20 southbound scheduled to leave at 1022 arrives one minute early, the assistant train dispatcher should   33._____

    A. hold run number 18 for one minute to make a *meet*
    B. merely hold the train until 1022
    C. ask the preceding time point if the train left early
    D. check whether the schedule time can be cut by one minute

34. Two locals and two expresses are scheduled to be rung off at exactly the same time at   34._____

    A. 1120   B. 1112   C. 1110   D. 1100

35. The number of different motormen who stop at station C between 1035 and 1140, inclusive, is   35._____

    A. 25   B. 24   C. 21   D. 18

36. The total number of different crew tricks shown in the northbound local runs is   36._____

    A. 10   B. 12   C. 15   D. 22

37. The crew which has time for lunch at the north local terminal is on run number 37._____

    A. 11   B. 15   C. 19   D. 23

38. One tour which probably clears at the south express terminal is run number 38._____

    A. 24   B. 20   C. 16   D. 12

39. If all northbound local trains stopping at station C from 1020 to 1120, inclusive, have 8 cars, the total number of cars on these trains is 39._____

    A. 48   B. 64   C. 96   D. 128

40. The terminal which is FARTHEST from station C is the destination of the 40._____

    A. northbound locals   B. northbound expresses
    C. southbound locals   D. southbound expresses

41. The total number of northbound locals scheduled to be at a ten-minute headway during the period shown is 41._____

    A. 3   B. 5   C. 7   D. 8

42. The transit system divisions that have stations at the New York Coliseum are the 42._____

    A. BMT and IRT   B. IND and BMT
    C. IRT and IND   D. IND, BMT, and IRT

43. A train is bound for the yard if both of its front marker lights are 43._____

    A. red   B. green   C. white   D. yellow

44. Block signals which are normally at danger and which enforce train operation at a predetermined reduced speed are classified as _____ signals. 44._____

    A. G.T.   B. S.T.   C. approach   D. dwarf

45. Because the latest types of cars used in the subway have dynamic brakes, 45._____

    A. higher speeds are attained
    B. less steel dust is deposited
    C. weight of cars is reduced
    D. longer trains have become practical

46. The only rapid transit line which crosses the Harlem River on a bridge is the _____ Line. 46._____

    A. Pelham Bay Park   B. Woodlawn
    C. Dyre Avenue   D. Van Cortlandt Park

47. The model board above a unit-lever interlocking machine indicates 47._____

    A. which tracks are occupied by trains
    B. the destinations of approaching trains
    C. which signals are clear
    D. which routes are set up

48. There is NO under-river subway tunnel from Manhattan at _____ Street. 48._____

    A. Whitehall   B. Fulton   C. 23rd   D. 42nd

49. When filling out a lost property form, an assistant dispatcher need NOT record 49._____

    A. the name of the person turning in the article
    B. a description of the article
    C. an estimate of the value of the article
    D. the place found or the time turned in

50. Bulletin orders are sometimes reissued without change and are marked as reissues of previous orders. The purpose of this procedure is USUALLY to 50._____

    A. replace worn-out orders on bulletin boards
    B. remind employees that the order is still important
    C. supersede prior conflicting bulletins
    D. remind employees that supervision is alert and active

KEY (CORRECT ANSWERS)

1. B	11. D	21. D	31. A	41. D
2. B	12. C	22. A	32. C	42. C
3. D	13. B	23. C	33. B	43. D
4. A	14. B	24. C	34. D	44. A
5. C	15. C	25. A	35. D	45. B
6. C	16. C	26. C	36. A	46. D
7. C	17. B	27. B	37. B	47. A
8. A	18. B	28. B	38. C	48. C
9. C	19. B	29. D	39. A	49. C
10. A	20. D	30. A	40. D	50. B

TEST 3

DIRECTIONS: Each question or incomplete statement is followed by several suggested answers or completions. Select the one that BEST answers the question or completes the statement. *PRINT THE LETTER OF THE CORRECT ANSWER IN THE SPACE AT THE RIGHT.*

1. Rule 35(e) reads as follows: *Unless otherwise directed by proper authority, trains must be operated in accordance with the schedule.* The PROPER authority referred to in this rule is the

    A. chief schedule maker
    B. road trainmaster
    C. desk trainmaster
    D. motorman instructor

    1.____

2. A motorman operating a 10-car train of *R* cars with two conductors reports failure of the motorman's indication.
He should be instructed to

    A. discharge passengers immediately and remove the train from service
    B. wait for the road car inspector and then proceed with the inspector on board
    C. continue with the train in service using buzzer signals after a clear understanding with the first position conductor
    D. wait for the road car inspector and have the indication repaired before proceeding

    2.____

3. There is NO East River bridge at _____ Street.

    A. 42nd   B. Delancey   C. 59th   D. Canal

    3.____

4. Car information is entered on Trips and Mileage *Data*. Sheets in different colored pencil by the midnight, A.M., and P.M. forces. The color which is required to be used for such purpose by the midnight forces is

    A. green   B. red   C. blue   D. black

    4.____

5. If a train dispatcher is required to work one hour in excess of his regularly scheduled hours on any day, he will receive for this work

    A. no extra pay or extra time off
    B. pay for one and one-half hours at his regular rate
    C. pay for one hour at his regular rate
    D. one hour off with pay

    5.____

6. A CORRECT statement according to the rules is that speed of trains

    A. is restricted to 15 M.P.H. over all diverging routes unless otherwise indicated
    B. on straight main-line tracks is restricted to 35 M.P.H.
    C. in under-river tubes between shafts is restricted to 15 M.P.H. when operating around sharp curves
    D. entering terminals unless otherwise restricted must not exceed 15 M.P.H.

    6.____

7. One of the prescribed duties of a train dispatcher is to

   A. supervise all employees in train and yard service in his section
   B. check the performance of train crews on the road
   C. authorize the making up of extra trains when necessary
   D. prepare timetables and crew sheets

8. An express train which has been diverted to the local track is required to stop

   A. at all stations if the schedule can be maintained
   B. at all stations regardless of whether the schedule can be maintained
   C. only at express stations unless otherwise directed
   D. only at the stations which are time points

9. Train dispatchers should be qualified to operate all interlocking towers in their sections. The statement which is NOT a reason for this requirement is that a dispatcher may have to

   A. operate any of these towers in an emergency
   B. supervise the towermen in his section
   C. answer questions of a relief towerman about a tower
   D. qualify new towermen in his section

10. If a series of automatic signals were to have the S.T. feature added, the purpose would PROBABLY be to

    A. compensate for changes in passenger loads
    B. make the signals lever-controlled
    C. make it possible to operate at a closer headway
    D. reduce the speed of trains

11. The proper standard symbol to use on a train register sheet to indicate that a certain car has been cut from a train at the terminal is to draw a _____ the car number.

    A. circle around   B. bracket at each end of
    C. straight line under   D. box around

Questions 12-22.

DIRECTIONS: Questions 12 through 22 are based on the portion of the Line M timetable and the motormen's work programs shown on the following page. Refer to this information in answering these questions. Line M is a two-track line without branch lines. Assume that operations proceed without delays unless otherwise noted. An X in any box indicates that an entry has been intentionally omitted because it can readily be determined from the data given.

3 (#3)

TIMETABLE - LINE M - DAILY

Aide St. Lv.	Bass St. Lv.	Cape St. Lv.	Flint Ave. Arr.	Flint Ave. Lv.	Cape St. Lv.	Bass St. Lv.	Aide St. Arr.	Aide St. Lv.
816	826	839	850	854	905	918	928	936
822	832	845	856	900	911	924	934	942
828	838	851	902	906	917	930	940	X
834	844	857	908	912	923	936	946	954
924	934	947	958	1002	1013	1026	1036	1044
930	940	953	1004	1008	1019	1032	1042	1050
936	946	959	1010	1014	1025	1038	1048	1056
942	952	1005	1016	1020	1031	1044	1054	1102

MOTORMEN'S WORK PROGRAMS - LINE M - DAILY

Run No.	M/M	Report Time	Report Place	Aide St. Lv.	Flint Ave. Arr.	Flint Ave. Lv.	Aide St. Arr.	Aide St. Lv.	Flint Ave. Arr.	Flint Ave. Lv.	Aide St. Arr.	Relieved Time	Relieved Place	Time on Duty Act.	Time on Duty Allow
137	Gard	149	Aide	204	238	243	317	328	402	407	441			X	800
				452	526	531	605	650	724	731	805				
				828	902	906	940					940	Aide	X	800
138	John	201	Aide	216	250	255	329	340	414	419	453				
				504	538	543	617	700	734	741	815				
				834	908	912	946					946	Aide	745	800
144	Lee	251	Aide	306	340	345	419	430	504	509	543				
				554	628	633	707	746	820	826	900				
				912	946	950	1024					1024	Aide	733	800
145	Nile	X	Aide	317	351	356	430	441	515	520	554				
				605	639	644	718	816	850	854	928				
				942	1016	1020	1054					1054	Aide	751	800

12. The number of round trips in Lee's tour of duty is

    A. 4   B. 5   C. 8   D. 10

13. The motorman whose tour gives him the MOST time for his lunch period is

    A. Gard   B. John   C. Lee   D. Nile

14. On a day when Lee is delayed by traffic conditions so that he clears twenty-seven minutes late, he is entitled, according to the Working Conditions, to be paid at his regular rate of pay for

    A. 8 hours
    B. 8 hours, 18 minutes
    C. 8 hours, 27 minutes
    D. 8 hours, 41 minutes

15. If Nile is delayed by traffic conditions so that he clears twenty-seven minutes late, he is entitled, according to the Working Conditions, to be paid at his regular rate of pay for

    A. 8 hours
    B. 8 hours, 18 minutes
    C. 8 hours, 27 minutes
    D. 8 hours, 41 minutes

16. Assuming no cuts or adds, the cars which leave Aide St. at 816 will later arrive at Flint at

    A. 854   B. 936   C. 1048   D. 1130

17. Because of an emergency, John was required to take out Gard's last trip from Aide St. To do this, John's relay time at Aide St. had to be cut to _____ minutes.

    A. 6   B. 13   C. 19   D. 23

18. Of the 14 intervals shown in the timetable leaving Aide St., the number covered by the four tours of duty shown in the work programs is

    A. 2   B. 3   C. 4   D. 5

19. The two motormen whose tours give them the MOST opportunities to speak to each other at Aide St. are

    A. Gard and John
    B. John and Lee
    C. Lee and Nile
    D. Nile and Gard

20. At 800, the dispatcher at Flint Ave. receives a telephone message for Lee, and promptly relays the message to the dispatcher at Aide St. Assuming no intermediate dispatching points, the EARLIEST that Lee can receive the message is

    A. 810   B. 815   C. 820   D. 825

21. Except for his reporting and lunch periods, the LONGEST time Lee has at Aide St. is _____ minutes.

    A. 10   B. 11   C. 12   D. 13

22. Gard's scheduled actual time on duty is _____ hrs., _____ min.

    A. 7; 17   B. 7; 45   C. 7; 51   D. 8; 0

23. When, due to an emergency or to failure of a motorman to report, it becomes necessary for a terminal dispatcher to fill a road trick with a member of his local force, first priority, according to latest instructions, MUST be given to the

    A. board motorman
    B. extra list men (no assignment)
    C. vacation relief man (no assignment)
    D. qualified switchman

24. Assume that the present timetable provides for 15 trains per hour on one track at a certain time point. If the timetable is changed to provide 24 trains per hour on this track, the average change in headway will be _____ minute(s).

    A. 1   B. 1 1/4   C. 1 1/2   D. 2 1/2

Questions 25-37.

DIRECTIONS: Questions 25 through 37 are based on the track layout and table of car service shown below. Consult this sketch and table in answering these questions.

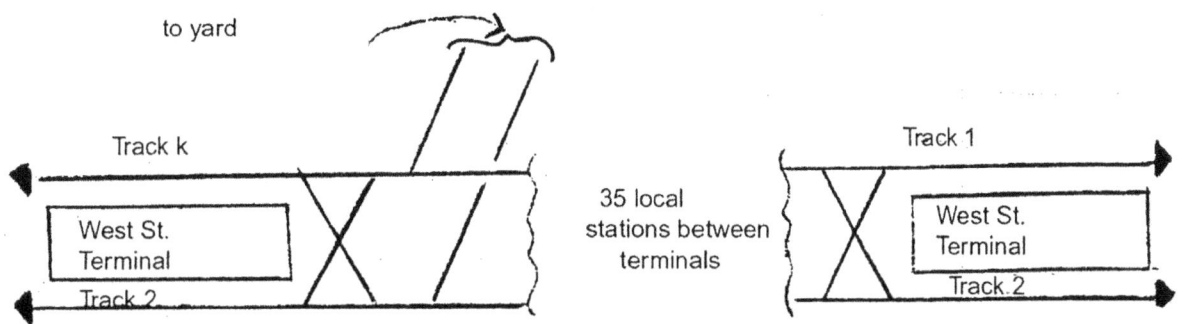

TRAIN SERVICE - WEST ST. TERMINAL - WEEKDAYS

ARRIVING				LEAVING			
From	To	Headway (Minutes)	No. Cars	From	To	Headway (Minutes)	No. Cars
12:25 AM	1:25 AM	10	6	12:03 AM	12:51 AM	12	6
1:36	3:00	12	6	1:06	4:36	15	4
3:15	6:45	15	4	4:48	5:48	10	6
6:57	7:57	10	6	5:56	6:28	8	8
8:05	8:37	8	8	6:33	8:58	5	10
8:42	11:07	5	10	9:05	9:40	7	10
1:14	11:49	7	10	9:47	2:06 PM	7	8
1:56	4:15 PM	7	8	2:11 PM	3:06	5	8
4:20 PM	5:15	5	8	3:11	5:11	5	10
5:20	7:20	5	10	5:18	6:00	7	10
7:27	8:09	7	10	6:07	6:56	7	8
8:16	9:05	7	8	7:06	10:06	10	8
9:15	12:15 AM	10	8	10:16	11:16	10	6
				11:27	11:51	12	6

NOTES:
1. The line between West St. and East St. is a 2-track line without any branch lines.
2. Two cars are cut off the 2:12 AM arrival at West St. and the remaining 4 cars dispatched to the road at 2:21 AM.
3. The relay time at East St. is 9 minutes for all trains.
4. Trains which remain in passenger service lay over at West St. for not less than 5 minutes nor more than twice the shorter headway (arriving or leaving) in effect at any particular time.
5. The scheduled terminal-to-terminal running time is exactly one hour.
6. All trains are made up of *married pairs*.
7. All operations proceed without delays unless otherwise stated.

25. The TOTAL number of trains in passenger service at 12:00 noon is 25.____
   A. 18   B. 20   C. 22   D. 24

26. The number of men needed to just crew all the trains in passenger service at 8:45 AM is 26.____
   A. 42   B. 48   C. 56   D. 60

27. The total number of put-ins between 5:00 AM and 9:00 AM is 27.____
   A. 10   B. 12   C. 14   D. 17

28. Not counting any trains which may be at the terminals, the number of westbound trains that should be between West St. and East St. at 2:00 PM is 28.____
   A. 8   B. 9   C. 10   D. 11

29. The number of *married pairs* that MUST be cut off trains arriving at West St. between 9:45 AM and 10:45 AM is 29.____
   A. 7   B. 9   C. 14   D. 18

30. The TOTAL number of cars that are adds (not including put-ins) from 3:00 PM to 5:30 PM is 30.____
   A. 22 or 24   B. 44 or 46   C. 68 or 70   D. 84 or 86

31. The time interval between the last A.M. put-in and the first A.M. lay-up is CLOSEST to _____ minutes. 31.____
   A. 15   B. 30   C. 45   D. 60

32. The average schedule time per station is NEAREST to _____ seconds. 32.____
   A. 94   B. 97   C. 100   D. 103

33. If the intermediate stations are uniformly spaced, then if a train is stopped in a station at the time of minimum headway, his follower should be _____ station behind. 33.____
   A. stopped at the 3rd
   B. in motion between the 3rd and 2nd
   C. stopped at the 2nd
   D. in motion between the 2nd and 1st

34. Cars are NOT added or cut, nor are trains put in, or laid up, at or about 34.____
   A. 1:00 AM   B. 7:00 AM   C. 1:00 PM   D. 7:00 PM

35. The TOTAL number of *married pairs* required to maintain the service on this line, allowing five percent for gap trains and shopping, is 35.____
   A. 135   B. 142   C. 270   D. 284

36. If the dispatcher at West St. is notified at 3:50 AM that the train scheduled to arrive at 4:00 AM will be 10 minutes late because of a temporary blockade, the dispatcher should 36.____

A. dispatch his gap train on time and lay up the delayed train on arrival
B. dispatch the delayed train and its leader 5 minutes late each
C. dispatch all trains on time
D. call the desk trainmaster for orders

37. The total number of scheduled eastbound intervals in a 24-hour period is 37.____

    A. 176 B. 187 C. 198 D. 209

38. If a special inspector identifies himself and asks for information about a particular motor- 38.____
    man from the train dispatcher at a terminal, the dispatcher should, in every case,

    A. give the information and cooperate to the best of his knowledge
    B. request the special inspector to show written authorization
    C. refer his questions to the trainmaster
    D. refer the special inspector to the crew dispatcher

39. According to outstanding Instructions, the train dispatcher who observes an illuminated 39.____
    smoke detector light must FIRST notify the

    A. trainmaster   B. telephone maintainer
    C. towerman   D. signal maintainer

40. The speed setting of a series of G.T. signals on a 1-mile stretch of track between succes- 40.____
    sive express stops is changed from 30 M.P.H. to 35 M.P.H. The change in running time
    as a result of this change in speed is NEAREST to _____ seconds.

    A. 7 B. 12 C. 17 D. 22

41. The running time between two local terminals is 40 minutes. If the average speed of the 41.____
    trains on this run is 15 M.P.H., the distance between these terminals is APPROXI-
    MATELY _____ miles.

    A. 8 B. 10 C. 12 D. 14

42. If a train dispatcher pulls an emergency alarm in the subway, it will cause the removal of 42.____
    power from the third rails in the vicinity and also

    A. start the exhaust fans and sound an alarm in the trainmaster's office
    B. sound an alarm in the nearest fire house and turn on the emergency car lights
    C. sound an alarm in the trainmaster's office and cause all the signals in the area to
       go to danger
    D. start the exhaust fans and connect the adjacent telephone to the trainmaster's
       office

43. It is common knowledge among railroad men that a speed of 15 miles per hour is exactly 43.____
    equal to 22 feet per second. In accordance with this rule, select the FASTEST of the fol-
    lowing speeds:

    A. 70 feet per second   B. 50 miles per hour
    C. 0.9 mile per minute   D. 4500 feet per minute

44. A towerman calls the attention of the dispatcher to the fact that a certain section of track is occupied by the Sperry Rail Car, but that the model board does not indicate occupancy of the track section. The cause of this condition is MOST likely

    A. a broken rail
    B. the shortness of the track section
    C. an incorrect route set-up
    D. the lightness of the rail car

45. Route request buttons have been installed at certain home signals. These buttons are to be operated by the motorman when the home signal is at danger and no call-on is displayed, or when an improper route is displayed. The PRINCIPAL advantage of such route request buttons over the use of the train whistle is that, with the buttons, the motorman

    A. need not come to a stop to request a route
    B. must come to a full stop to request a route
    C. is less likely to make an error
    D. is giving a more precise indication

46. The train on which you are riding takes 24 seconds to go from Signal M4-630 to M4-617 (Signal 6304/M to Signal 6174/M in IRT nomenclature). The average speed of the train between these signals was MOST probably in the range from _____ M.P.H.

    A. 20 to 25 B. 25 to 30 C. 30 to 35 D. 35 to 40

47. A recent bulletin states, in part, that windows of unoccupied motormen's cabs must be kept closed at all times. The reason given in the bulletin for this requirement is that closed cab windows help to

    A. prevent vandalism
    B. keep the cab clean
    C. prevent use of the cab for immoral purposes
    D. keep the cab dry

48. When a certain job on a track is finished and the flagging protection is removed, the color of the lamp or flag to be removed last is

    A. white B. yellow C. green D. red

49. On a portion of track where one-block-overlap automatic signals are used, the indications of the three signals immediately behind a train, starting with the one NEAREST the train, are

    A. red, yellow, yellow
    B. red, red, red
    C. red, yellow, green
    D. red, red, yellow

50. Certain service cars must never be placed on the open end of a train. Based on your knowledge of service car equipment, you should know that this restriction applies to service cars which are NOT equipped with

    A. marker lights
    B. hand brakes
    C. automatic couplers
    D. trip cocks

KEY (CORRECT ANSWERS)

1. C	11. B	21. C	31. B	41. B
2. A	12. B	22. C	32. C	42. A
3. A	13. D	23. B	33. A	43. C
4. D	14. A	24. C	34. C	44. D
5. D	15. B	25. B	35. B	45. D
6. D	16. D	26. C	36. C	46. D
7. A	17. B	27. D	37. B	47. A
8. C	18. C	28. B	38. A	48. C
9. D	19. A	29. B	39. D	49. D
10. C	20. C	30. B	40. C	50. D

EXAMINATION SECTION
TEST 1

DIRECTIONS: Each question or incomplete statement is followed by several suggested answers or completions. Select the one that BEST answers the question or completes the statement. *PRINT THE LETTER OF THE CORRECT ANSWER IN THE SPACE AT THE RIGHT.*

1. As a station supervisor, if you think of a means for controlling passengers at the foot of a station escalator, your BEST procedure would be to

   A. get the opinion of the subway employees assigned to the station
   B. discuss it with an assistant supervisor of the elevator and escalator department
   C. ask your supervisor for the assignment of sufficient personnel to give the plan a trial before recommending it
   D. consider the idea carefully before recommending it

1._____

2. Before giving a conductor on the train the proper hand signal to close the doors, the conductor assigned to platform duty should ascertain whether

   A. the scheduled time for departure has arrived
   B. all waiting passengers are aboard
   C. a connecting train is approaching
   D. all doors are opened

2._____

3. Courtesy to passengers is constantly impressed on subway employees *mainly* to

   A. improve public relations
   B. increase the use of subways by the public
   C. minimize operating difficulties
   D. assure the safety of the passengers

3._____

4. An excited passenger, just inside the turnstiles, calls out something to the railroad clerk in the booth which he cannot understand.
   The *best* course of action for the clerk to take would be to

   A. ignore the passenger until he comes over to the booth
   B. close the booth and go over to the turnstiles to investigate
   C. tell the passenger he will get help for him
   D. tell the passenger to calm down so he can understand

4._____

5. A thorough knowledge of the schedule of working conditions for employees in the station department will help an assistant station supervisor to know

   A. how to tell whether a porter is doing a satisfactory job
   B. when one of his subordinates should be reprimanded
   C. if certain of his duties can be delegated to one of his subordinates
   D. what monetary rights his subordinates have

5._____

6. A station supervisor will find that it is sometimes more effective to warn a subordinate than to institute action for more severe punishment, because

   A. the warning is less severe
   B. the punishment is often inappropriate
   C. the warning may produce a more cooperative attitude
   D. a warning always creates a better impression than punishment

6._____

45

7. One of your workers, when reporting to work, claims he is not feeling well. After working just over an hour, he requests permission to go home as he is feeling worse. He refuses to have medical attention, and, since he is obviously sick, he is allowed to leave.
   In this case, the time charged against his sick leave allowance should be

   A. 1/4 day   B. 1/2 day   C. 3/4 day   D. a full day

8. CO_2 type fire extinguishers are mounted on tunnel walls. In order to have them available for any emergency it is especially essential that

   A. they be frequently replaced
   B. they be periodically inspected
   C. only designated persons should use them
   D. prompt notice be given whenever they are used

9. One of your railroad clerks asks you to grant him a minor privilege. In granting or denying such a request, you should consider

   A. that all such requests should be denied
   B. the clerk's seniority
   C. the merits of the case
   D. that it is bad for employees morale to grant a request of this nature

10. The revenue department is nost desirous that railroad clerks be very careful when handling revenue because errors in bagging

    A. are difficult to detect
    B. increase the department's work load
    C. reflect on the railroad clerks honesty
    D. result in erroneous reports of daily receipts

11. A conductor assigned to platform duty is expected to

    A. normally remain on duty until relieved
    B. prevent anyone from loitering in or around the change booth
    C. gently push a person into a crowded car so the doors can close
    D. stop people running from trains to stairways

12. Certain types of lost property found on the transit system should be held for 12 hours and then either sold or destroyed. Such an article would be a

    A. broken umbrella   B. bottle of liquor
    C. basket of fruit   D. thermos bottle full of milk

13. As a result of a recent safety bulletin, a certain railroad porter has taken upon himself the duty of thoroughly inspecting his assigned territory for any condition which he thinks requires any repairs or painting and is constantly reporting such information to the station supervisor.
    The most *effective* means of dealing with such a situation is to

    A. have a talk with the porter and explain just what is expected of him
    B. disregard the reports until the porter realizes that he is making a nuisance of himself
    C. recommend giving him a special assignment of inspecting all the stations under the supervision of this assistant station supervisor
    D. get tough with the porter and insist he pay more attention to his assigned work

14. If a new method of bagging revenue were to be started at a certain station, the station supervisor desiring to minimize errors should   14.____

    A. know that considerable time may be required for employees to become familiar with the procedure
    B. realize that frequent mistakes are possible
    C. keep this station under close supervision
    D. do the initial bagging himself

15. A certain cleaner, while working under your supervision, swept the station very thoroughly when it was swept but did not sweep as often as necessary. Shortly after picking a different station his new station supervisor asks your opinion of the cleaner.   15.____
    Your *best* course of action would be to

    A. point out the man's good qualities only
    B. point out the man's faults only
    C. point out both his good and his poor characteristics
    D. avoid committing yourself in order to give him a chance at a new station

QUESTIONS 16-21.

Questions 16 to 21 are based on the situation described below. Consider the facts given in this situation when answering these questions.

Assume that at a certain subway station a complete traffic count is to be taken on May 26th for a period of 24 hours. A total of 15 employees are assigned to make the count under the general supervision of a station supervisor, assisted by 3 "light duty" train operators.

16. The verbal instructions given to the assigned counters by the station supervisor should be as brief and concise as possible in order to   16.____

    A. avoid confusing the counters
    B. emphasize the importance of the instructions
    C. get the count started as soon as possible
    D. be effective

17. The most *probable* reason for assigning the motormen as assistants is that they   17.____

    A. have a higher title than the counters
    B. are experienced in such work
    C. can be depended on to prepare reports correctly
    D. receive more training than the other employees

18. If the largest number of counters are assigned to work between 5 a.m. and 8 a.m., this would *most likely* indicate that the station is located   18.____

    A. in a residential area   B. in a manufacturing district
    C. at a shopping center   D. at a railroad terminal

19. To accomplish the purpose for which it is intended, such a traffic count should be conducted

    A. frequently
    B. by experienced people
    C. with accuracy
    D. only at congested stations

20. The reason for assigning so many employees to this task is *most likely* due to

    A. their inexperience
    B. the number of people using this station
    C. the impracticable way in which this count is taken
    D. the physical layout of the station

21. The *least probable* reason for conducting such a count is to

    A. determine when the station is the most crowded
    B. determine if additional turnstiles are needed
    C. make a comparison between the number of people leaving the station and those entering the station
    D. determine the "flow" of passengers at certain stairways

22. Many accidents could be prevented if employees remember that safety rules

    A. will be strictly enforced
    B. should be learned
    C. are often used and based on previous accidents
    D. should be obeyed

23. All employee training courses are beneficial to the system because such courses

    A. tend to increase employee efficiency
    B. prepare employees for promotional examinations
    C. are given by people well acquainted with the work
    D. increase the interest of new employees

24. A station agent in a booth is notified by the station supervisor that a special relief is being sent to permit the clerk to come to his office.
    When the relief arrives, it is *most important* that the station agent should

    A. make certain the booth is locked before he leaves
    B. not admit the man to the booth unless certain of his identity
    C. notify his superior of the relief's arrival
    D. inform the station porter that he is going to the office

25. A station agent noticing that a post light cannot be turned off should make an immediate report to his office *primarily* to

    A. have repairs made promptly
    B. avoid criticism by his superior
    C. find out what the trouble is
    D. determine if this defect was previously reported

26. A station agent may exchange tokens for as many as 4 regular cash fare tickets when presented by a passenger, but is only permitted to exchange one token for a single special (red) cash fare ticket issued by the Board of Education for an elementary school pupil.
The *most probable* reason for limiting the exchange to a single ticket issued for school pupils is to

   A. minimize the possibility of the school tickets being used illegally
   B. prevent the school tickets from being stolen
   C. insure that the school ticket is only used by the one to whom issued
   D. enable the railroad clerk to check that the school ticket had been regularly issued

27. A station agent in a change booth should be most interested in the fact that a child under 6 years traveling with an adult is

   A. liable to break away from the adult and dash under the turnstile
   B. not to occupy a seat to the exclusion of an adult
   C. the responsibility of the adult he accompanies
   D. to be carried free of charge

28. To frustrate holdups, station agents are instructed

   A. as to the time holdups usually occur
   B. to be careful lest perpetrators be armed
   C. as to the general appearance of holdup men
   D. to keep booth doors locked

29. The most significant argument against making it compulsory for civil service employees to attend a training course is

   A. trainees must be receptive if training is to be successful
   B. most training requires additional time and expense on the part of the trainee
   C. unwilling trainees will be penalized in any event by non-promotion
   D. training is highly desirable, but not absolutely essential, for adequate job performance

30. A station employee should NOT enter upon the subway tracks without first

   A. notifying another employee where he is going
   B. checking to make sure that no trains are coming
   C. having someone stationed to warn him of approaching trains
   D. obtaining the required flagging protection

KEY (CORRECT ANSWERS)

1.	D	16.	A
2.	B	17.	A
3.	A	18.	B
4.	D	19.	C
5.	D	20.	D
6.	C	21.	C
7.	C	22.	D
8.	D	23.	A
9.	C	24.	B
10.	B	25.	A
11.	A	26.	A
12.	C	27.	D
13.	A	28.	D
14.	C	29.	A
15.	C	30.	B

TEST 2

DIRECTIONS: Each question or incomplete statement is followed by several suggested answers or completions. Select the one that BEST answers the question or completes the statement. *PRINT THE LETTER OF THE CORRECT ANSWER IN THE SPACE AT THE RIGHT.*

QUESTIONS 1-10.

Questions 1-10 contain working schedules that refer to the column of time allowances shown below. Select the proper time allowance in the column which should be used with the working schedule given in each question.

Column of time allowances

A.	8 hr. 00 min.	M.	9 hr. 15 min.
B.	8 hr. 15 min.	O.	9 hr. 30 min.
C.	8 hr. 20 min.	P.	9 hr. 45 min.
D.	8 hr. 30 min.	S.	10 hr. 00 min.
E.	8 hr. 40 min.	T.	10 hr. 30 min.
H.	8 hr. 45 min.	V.	11 hr. 00 min.
J.	9 hr. 00 min.	X.	11 hr. 30 min.
K.	9 hr. 10 min.		

1. A railroad clerk reported at 8:00 A.M., was relieved at 11:30 A.M., resumed work at 11:55 A.M. and went home at 4:00 P.M. He was told to phone his office at 5:30 P.M. for possible emergency work. He did so but was told he was not needed. 1.____

2. A station employee reported at 3:00 P.M., was relieved for lunch at 7:00 P.M., resumed work at 7:30 P.M., and was relieved at 11:00 P.M. 2.____

3. A station employee reported at 8:00 A.M., was relieved for lunch at 12:15 P.M. and resumed work at 12:40 P.M. His relief failed to arrive at 4:00 P.M. as scheduled so he had to work until relieved at 4:30 P.M. 3.____

4. A cleaner reported at 8:00 A.M., went to lunch at 1:00 P.M., resumed work at 3:40 P.M., worked until 6:30 P.M. 4.____

5. A station employee reported at 6:00 A.M., was relieved at 11:30 A.M., resumed work at 12:00 Noon and was relieved at 2:00 P.M. He was told to come back at 4:00 P.M. for emergency work. When he did so, he was told he was not needed. 5.____

6. A cleaner reported at 6:00 A.M., went to lunch at 10:30 A.M., resumed work at 10:40 A.M. because of an emergency, and worked until 2:00 P.M. 6.____

7. A station employee reported at 5:00 A.M., was relieved at 9:45 A.M., resumed work at 10:10 A.M. Relief failed to arrive at 1:00 P.M. as scheduled, so he worked until relieved at 1:50 P.M. 7.____

8. A station employee reported at 8:00 A.M., was relieved at 11:45 A.M., resumed at 12:15 P.M., and was relieved at 4:00 P.M. He reported back as directed at 5:30 P.M., put to work, and released at 6:30 P.M. 8.____

9. A station employee reported at 11:00 P.M., was relieved at 4:00 A.M. and resumed work at 4:30 A.M. Relief failed to arrive at 7:00 A.M. as scheduled, so he had to work until relieved at 8:10 A.M. 9.____

51

10. A cleaner reported at 7:00 A.M., went to lunch at 12:30 P.M., resumed at 1:45 P.M., and worked until 4:15 P.M.

10.___

11. One of your cleaners was injured as a result of slipping on a wet spot on the station platform. This type of accident would *most likely* be classified as due to

    A. defective equipment
    B. poor housekeeping
    C. physical condition
    D. proper safety appliances not used

11.___

12. A cleaner, who is a habitual complainer, presents a grievance which has some merit. As a station supervisor, you should handle this grievance by

    A. ignoring it
    B. recommending unfavorable action
    C. referring it to your supervisor
    D. adjusting it if possible

12.___

13. A characteristic which a station supervisor should consider most desirable in his subordinates is the

    A. willingness to report back to the assistant supervisor all disparaging remarks made by the employees
    B. desire to put in as much overtime as possible
    C. ability to refrain from talking with passengers
    D. ability to properly carry out assignments with a minimum of instructions

13.___

14. Air raid sirens are located at various stations on the transit system. Railroad clerks at these locations are instructed to note the time at which test signals are received at their location. The main reason for those time notations is

    A. to test time clocks on the system
    B. that the sirens throughout the city be synchronized
    C. too see if the railroad clerks are alert
    D. that the same signal is received at all locations

14.___

15. It would be poor supervision if a station supervisor

    A. consulted his supervisor on personnel problems
    B. made it a policy to avoid criticism of his subordinates in front of passengers
    C. allowed a cooling-off period of several days before giving one of his subordinates a deserved reprimand
    D. asked an experienced porter for his opinion of a suggested method for cleaning tile

15.___

16. You believe that a conductor assigned to platform duty at one of your stations shirks his duty whenever possible. To ascertain the validity of your belief it would be *best* for you to

    A. make several unscheduled visits to the location
    B. question the railroad clerk on duty at the station
    C. question the conductor to see if he knows what his duties are
    D. dispatch another employee to check on the conductor

16.___

17. A station supervisor criticizing a cleaner's work expresses disappointment, stating that not only is his work entirely unsatisfactory, but that his accident record is also bad.
The station supervisor's method of handling this situation would usually be considered

   A. poor; the cleaner should have been asked why his work was poor
   B. poor; some favorable comment should have been made at the same time
   C. good; it is advisable to keep this type of interview as short as possible
   D. good; the cleaner will realize that his work will have to improve if he is to keep his job

18. Whenever an employee under your supervision has an accident on the job, you, as a station supervisor, are *required* to

   A. make sure that the employee prepares and submits an accident report before the completion of his tour of duty
   B. prepare and submit a "supervisory accident report" before the completion of your tour of duty
   C. immediately investigate and give an oral report to your supervisor
   D. recommend means to prevent a repetition of the accident

19. At stations where additional personnel are required to sell fares, the exact location where the seller stands is determined primarily by

   A. its proximity to the change booth
   B. the lighting in the station
   C. the line of flow of traffic
   D. the number of passengers using the station

20. When a bulletin order is reissued without change, the purpose of this *usually* is to

   A. supersede prior bulletins
   B. stress its importance
   C. make sure the order reaches all bulletin boards
   D. replace lost copies

21. The *most* effective approach a station supervisor can pursue in transmitting a controversial order to his subordinates would be to state the order and

   A. briefly justify the controversial parts
   B. invite comments
   C. hold an open discussion on it
   D. explain that you expect it to be strictly obeyed

22. The *most* important reason for answering fully and completely all questions asked on accident reports is that

   A. experience has shown these questions to be necessary
   B. similar accidents will be eliminated in the future
   C. otherwise the safety committee will not be able to classify the accident
   D. it entirely eliminates the need for further investigation

23. If a station supervisor were to encounter the following conditions in the subway, the most dangerous one of them would be

    A. a flooded subway stairway as a result of heavy downpour of rain
    B. a subway car door which only opens half way at station steps
    C. crowding at the entrance to the subway escalator at the train platform level
    D. a newspaper delivery employee throwing bundles of papers off a local train at two adjacent stations

24. Assume you are preparing a report recommending a change in station cleaning procedures. It is most important that the report contain information as to

    A. when the new procedure could be put into effect
    B. whether the new procedure has already been tried
    C. the superiority of the new procedure
    D. origin of the new procedure

25. Some orders to station agents are issued orally by the station supervisor rather than by bulletin. This is because the subject matter of the verbal orders

    A. refers to less important matters
    B. is usually of local nature
    C. contains many details
    D. requires less effort to compose

26. A cleaner complains to his superior that the cleaner he relieves frequently stops to talk with passengers, and as a result, does not complete his work properly.
    The *most likely* conclusion would be that the porter complained of

    A. should be assigned to another location
    B. is popular with the passengers at his station
    C. is not interested in his work
    D. is lazy

27. Installation of well-designed machines capable of vending more than one fare at a time would be of greatest value to the operation of the subway system mainly because they would tend to

    A. replace railroad clerks
    B. eliminate errors
    C. alleviate congestion
    D. decrease necessary supervision

28. It is *most nearly* correct to say that

    A. employees who are thoroughly acquainted with the rules are most careful
    B. accidents usually result from carelessness
    C. proper supervision insures carefullness of employees
    D. a careful employee never has an accident

29. To avoid errors in station entrance computations, turnstile meters

    A. must be read at a definite time
    B. are placed on each turnstile
    C. have large and clear numbers
    D. require adequate maintenance

30. If a station agent was to see a passenger fall down a flight of stairs, his *first* action should be to

   A. request the cleaner to examine the stairs
   B. determine the cause of the accident
   C. call his office
   D. ascertain injuries

KEY (CORRECT ANSWERS)

1.	J	16.	A
2.	A	17.	B
3.	D	18.	B
4.	E	19.	C
5.	S	20.	B
6.	D	21.	A
7.	J	22.	A
8.	O	23.	D
9.	P	24.	C
10.	A	25.	B
11.	C	26.	C
12.	D	27.	C
13.	D	28.	B
14.	B	29.	A
15.	C	30.	D

EXAMINATION SECTION
TEST 1

DIRECTIONS: Each question or incomplete statement is followed by several suggested answers for completions. Select the one that BEST answers the question or completes the statement. *PRINT THE LETTER OF THE CORRECT ANSWER IN THE SPACE AT THE RIGHT.*

1. Good supervision requires that the station supervisor visit his assigned stations

    A. on a fixed schedule only
    B. as many times a day as possible
    C. only when trouble develops
    D. at random as well as regular intervals

2. At a subway station located in the financial district, a station supervisor would normally expect the GREATEST concentration of passenger traffic to occur from

    A. 6:30 A.M. to 8:00 A.M.   B. 7:30 A.M. to 8:30 A.M.
    C. 4:00 P.M. to 5:30 P.M.   D. 5:30 P.M. to 7:30 P.M.

3. The LEAST important reason for the requirement that all accidents on the transit system must be promptly investigated is that such investigation help to

    A. settle claims promptly
    B. fix responsibility
    C. set up a regular routine
    D. prevent similar accidents in the future

4. Two porters are to be assigned to a special cleaning job at a remote location. By placing the one with the better record in charge, the assistant supervisor will

    A. be showing good judgment
    B. know that the job will require no supervision on his part
    C. be following standard policy
    D. not be criticized if the job is poorly done

5. The BEST assurance a station supervisor can have that a railroad clerk knows how to do his work is if the clerk

    A. makes few mistakes   B. is cooperative
    C. works quickly   D. asks no questions

6. An accident involving an employee occurred on a job to which you had assigned two men.
   In questioning them separately to fix responsibility, you should be MAINLY interested in obtaining information pertaining to

    A. the ability and experience of each
    B. how well the other understood your instructions
    C. the manner in which the other performs his work
    D. what each was doing at the time the accident occurred

7. For the sake of safety while working under conditions which involve an element of danger, safety rules have been compiled

   A. to eliminate accidents
   B. to minimize time lost
   C. for the guidance of employees
   D. for avoiding dangerous assignments

8. Six porters can clean a certain tile wall in 3 hours. If two of the porters left one hour after starting work, the job would require _____ hours.

   A. 3 1/2   B. 4   C. 5   D. 9

9. Of the following the LEAST important element in good subway service is the

   A. size of the cars
   B. relative infrequency of breakdowns
   C. cleanliness of cars and stations
   D. courtesy of the employees

10. A report of an unusual occurrence is MOST likely to be accurate as to facts if written by the station supervisor

    A. before discussing matters with anyone
    B. right after the occurrence
    C. after discussion with the station supervisor
    D. the following day after thinking things over

11. The station supervisors on the 4 P.M. to midnight trick are responsible for the

    A. ordering and distribution of porter cleaning supplies
    B. storing of all special work train deliveries such as sawdust
    C. ordering and control of all stationery supplies used by railroad clerks
    D. for the collection of all torn and dirty revenue bags

12. If a porter reporting for duty falls and apparently sustains a broken leg, the station supervisor should immediately telephone the

    A. nearest T.A. clinic   B. first aid room
    C. supervisor's office   D. transit police

Questions 13-19.

DIRECTIONS: Questions 13 through 19 are based on the description of a special event given below. Refer to this description in answering these questions.

A special parade, on Thanksgiving Day, is to follow, for the first time, a line of march paralleling a nearby 4-track rapid transit line, and approximately 1 1/2 million spectators are anticipated. The parade is expected to take 3 hours to pass any given point and it will take 2 hours for any part of the parade to march from the beginning to the end of the route, starting near the Cliff Street express station at 10:00 A.M., marching north, and finishing near the Bank Street express station. There are 5 local stops between these points. No other rapid transit line is near the route of the parade although several surface lines cross the line of march. One terminal of the rapid transit line is about 30 minutes riding time from Cliff station via express, the other terminal is about 35 minutes riding time from Bank station via express, and the scheduled riding time from Cliff station to Bank station is 10 minutes via local and 6 minutes via express.

13. From the description of the event it is clear that one who wished to go from the Bank Street station to the Cliff Street station would have to travel

    A. north B. south C. east D. west

14. The employees of this rapid transit line should expect a large number of passengers to enter at Cliff Street station starting at about

    A. 11:00 A.M. B. 12:00 Noon C. 1:00 P.M. D. 3:00 P.M.

15. The employees of this rapid transit line should expect a large number of passengers to enter at Bank Street station starting at about

    A. 12:00 Noon B. 1:00 P.M.
    C. 2:00 P.M. D. 3:00 P.M.

16. The BEST place to make the count of passengers who come to watch the parade would be at

    A. the express stations B. the local stations
    C. Bank Street D. Cliff Street

17. If the local stops are uniformly spaced, the time it takes for any one part of the parade to march from one local station to the next is APPROXIMATELY _____ minutes.

    A. 10 B. 15 C. 20 D. 30

18. The riding time between the terminals of this line, via express, is

    A. 35 minutes B. 1 hour and 5 minutes
    C. 1 hour and 11 minutes D. 1 hour and 15 minutes

19. The BEST way to make the count of passengers who will probably use any particular station when the parade is over would be to

    A. assign personnel to all exits to count crowd leaving station
    B. count the number of tokens sold there to parade time
    C. take a turnstile count at that station until 12:00 P.M.
    D. estimate number of passengers exiting from trains stopping at that station

20. Ten car trains arrive on five minute intervals at a terminal station. Assuming that each car carries 120 passengers, the number of passengers exiting from the station in an hour is NEAREST to

    A. 8200 B. 12000 C. 14400 D. 16000

21. Of the following, the BEST way to have transit employees as a whole learn good safety habits is to

    A. penalize them with loss of pay for lost-time accidents
    B. let them learn through their own mistakes
    C. have them re-read the rules in their spare time
    D. offer prizes for the best safety records

4 (#1)

22. To keep errors in station entrance computations to a minimum, turnstile meters 22.___

   A. are placed on each turnstile
   B. must be read at definite times
   C. require much maintenance
   D. have large and clear numbers

23. One of the duties of station supervisors is to 23.___

   A. immediately report infractions of the rules which come to their attention
   B. check daily to see that railroad clerks and porters have ample supplies
   C. be responsible for any tools or equipment left by the turnstile section on any of the stations in his area
   D. make any changes in Station Department Instructions that are necessary

24. A cleaner complains to you that the porter he relieves does not complete his share of the 24.___
    work and that he has been informed that this is due to frequent and lengthy conversations with passengers.
    The LEAST likely conclusion would be that the cleaner complained of

   A. is well liked by the regular passengers at that station
   B. lives near the station
   C. is a responsible individual
   D. has had words with the cleaner turning him in

25. You have noticed that one of the cleaners at a station in your area is frequently in the tower 25.___
    at the end of the platform. He tells you that he is studying for the next railroad clerk promotion examination whenever he gets a chance.
    As station supervisor you should

   A. overlook this situation since it is temporary and reasonable
   B. inform him that he is never permitted in the tower
   C. transfer the man to a station in the area without a tower
   D. insist that he discontinue this practice during working hours

26. A recently appointed cleaner is assigned to duty under your supervision. 26.___
    Of the following, the MOST important thing to do is

   A. make sure he knows all the rules and regulations in detail
   B. acquaint him with traffic conditions at his station
   C. familiarize him with the schedule of working conditions for station employees
   D. take him on a tour of the station to which he will be assigned pointing out his duties

27. A systematic layout of work and proper assignment of men to a special job, by a 27.___
    supervisor, will NOT affect the

   A. amount of work to be done
   B. quality of the finished work
   C. time required to do the work
   D. kind of supervision needed in the performance of the work

28. A station supervisor, telephoning from an agent's booth located on a subway platform, hears a train whistle signal that sounds to him like *short-long-short*. If the signal is not repeated and the railroad clerk also is not sure of what he heard, the assistant station supervisor could logically conclude that he had heard part of a signal and that the motorman was actually signaling to alert

    A. people standing too close to the edge of the platform to move back
    B. station or police personnel that assistance is needed
    C. his conductor that the train will overrun or stop short of the station marker
    D. a car inspector to meet the train as something needs correction

29. A station having a total platform area of 22,575 sq. ft. is to be swept twice a week. If the average area that can be swept per hour is 5,250 sq. ft., the total time to be allotted for the twice-weekly sweeping is CLOSEST to _____ hours, _____ minutes.

    A. 4; 6   B. 4; 18   C. 8; 36   D. 9; 20

30. For three adjacent stations for the same period, the first requires twice as much sawdust as the second and the second twice as much as the third. If 14 bags of sawdust are to be properly distributed to these stations, the first station should receive _____ bags.

    A. 4   B. 6   C. 8   D. 10

KEY (CORRECT ANSWERS)

1.	D	16.	A
2.	C	17.	C
3.	C	18.	C
4.	A	19.	A
5.	A	20.	C
6.	D	21.	D
7.	C	22.	B
8.	B	23.	A
9.	A	24.	C
10.	B	25.	D
11.	C	26.	D
12.	D	27.	A
13.	B	28.	B
14.	C	29.	C
15.	D	30.	C

TEST 2

DIRECTIONS: Each question or incomplete statement is followed by several suggested answers or completions. Select the one that BEST answers the question or completes the statement. *PRINT THE LETTER OF THE CORRECT ANSWER IN THE SPACE AT THE RIGHT.*

1. The official published Rules and Regulations are LEAST useful in

   A. helping employees in the proper performance of their duties
   B. relieving supervisory employees of their responsibility
   C. providing a fair basis for any necessary disciplinary action
   D. encouraging safe practices

2. An employee of the transit system should give his name and badge number at the request of any passenger

   A. without argument after first trying to placate the passenger
   B. without delay or argument
   C. if a valid reason is given
   D. if the passenger insists strenuously

3. It is particularly important that assistant station supervisors be acquainted with the various rapid transit and surface lines in order to

   A. be able to move quickly to another point when necessary
   B. make the best disposition of passengers in case of blockade
   C. be able to make recommendations for better service
   D. generally answer passenger questions in this regard

4. Considerable time of supervision is required in investigating complaints by passengers against employees.
   The BEST overall solution to this problem is to

   A. have supervisors stress courtesy in public relations
   B. set up a central complaint bureau
   C. send a standard courteous answer and omit investigation
   D. investigate only the legitimate complaints

5. It would be POOR supervision on the part of a station supervisor if he

   A. consulted an experienced railroad clerk on an unusual problem
   B. made it a policy to avoid criticizing a man while another was present
   C. overlooked minor infractions of the rules on occasions
   D. allowed several days to elapse before giving one of his men a deserved reprimand

Questions 6-11.

DIRECTIONS: Questions 6 through 11 are based on the tabulation of Turnstile Readings shown below. Consult this tabulation in answering these questions. Note that booth No. 74 is open 24 hours a day, the clerk on the midnight tour reporting at 11:00 P.M.

TURNSTILE READING

BOOTH NO. 74 - WEST STREET STATION

Sunday - August 5.

HOUR	TURNSTILE NUMBER				
	1	2	3	4	5
5 AM	72583	00602	08390	22924	98832
6 AM	72650	00631	08437	22983	98893
7 AM	72705	00648	08472	23031	98945
8 AM	72747	00659	08501	23067	98958
9 AM	72779	00666	08524	23094	99025
10 AM	72805	00675	08535	23127	99064
11 AM	72853	00693	08544	23159	99129
12 NOON	72947	00718	08621	23240	99200
1 PM	73124	00796	08794	23394	99348
2 PM	73430	00958	09039	23660	99625
3 PM	74005	01366	09572	24161	00169
4 PM	74925	02032	10309	24961	00905
5 PM	76002	02906	11261	25898	01876
6 PM	77202	03873	12360	27010	03018
7 PM	78385	04953	13470	28128	04155
8 PM	79500	05847	14467	29137	05172
9 PM	80571	06705	15459	30126	06177

6. From the information given it is MOST probable that the 6.____

   A. most used stairway from the street is nearest turnstile #4
   B. #3 turnstile has just recently been put back in service
   C. entrance stairways are farthest from turnstiles #2, #3, and #4
   D. change booth is nearest turnstile #5

7. One of the listed turnstile readings which should be unlikely to appear on the regular 7.____
   Combined Railroad Clerks Daily Fare Report is

   A. 00602   B. 08437   C. 73430   D. 99625

8. If turnstile Nos. 3 and 4 had been closed during the entire period of the above tabulation 8.____
   while the total passenger traffic remained the same, and the passengers that would have
   used turnstiles Nos. 3 and 4 were divided equally among the other three turnstiles, the
   reading of turnstile #2 at 9 P.M. would have been

   A. 8390   B. 10860   C. 11462   D. 14271

9. If 40% of the passengers entering through these turnstiles on August 5th were registered in the six hours from 3 P.M. to 9 P.M., the total number of passengers registered this day was APPROXIMATELY

   A. 74500 B. 76000 C. 78000 D. 79500

10. The average number of passengers per minute using turnstile #2 during the busiest hour was NEAREST to

    A. 17 B. 18 C. 19 D. 20

11. The total number of passengers using turnstile #2 during the period from 5 P.M. to 8 P.M. was NEAREST to the number of passengers using turnstile

    A. #4 from 1 P.M. to 5 P.M.
    B. #3 from 8 A.M. to 5 P.M.
    C. #1 from 4 P.M. to 7 P.M.
    D. #5 from 4 P.M. to 7 P.M.

Questions 12-14.

DIRECTIONS: Questions 12 through 14 are based on the situation described below. Consider the facts given in this situation when answering these questions.

SITUATION

A new detergent that is to be added to water and the resulting mixture just wiped on any surface has been tested by the station department and appeared to be excellent. However you notice, after inspecting a large number of stations that your porters have cleaned with this detergent, that the surfaces cleaned are not as clean as they formerly were when the old method was used.

12. The MAIN reason for the station department testing the new detergent in the first place was to make certain that

    A. it was very simple to use
    B. a little bit would go a long way
    C. there was no stronger detergent on the market
    D. it was superior to anything formerly used

13. The MAIN reason that such a poor cleaning job resulted was MOST likely due to the

    A. porters being lax on the job
    B. detergent not being as good as expected
    C. incorrect amount of water being mixed with the detergent
    D. fact that the surfaces cleaned needed to be scrubbed

14. The reason for inspecting a number of stations was to

    A. determine whether all porters did the same job
    B. insure that the result of the cleaning job was the same in each location
    C. be certain that the detergent was used in each station inspected
    D. see whether certain surfaces cleaned better than others

15. A passenger asks you, the station supervisor, for directions on how to get to a certain place on the transit system.
If you do not know the answer you should tell the passenger

    A. that you do not know and try to direct him to someone who does know
    B. to look the answer up on the subway map posted at the station
    C. that only railroad clerks are able to give such directions
    D. to get aboard the next train and to ask the conductor

15.____

16. The Employee Suggestion Plan is beneficial to transit authority employees because they

    A. become more efficient employees after making a suggestion
    B. are certain to be rewarded for making suggestions
    C. have an opportunity to express their ideas with management
    D. acquaint themselves with the ideas of fellow employees

16.____

17. The LEAST valuable source of information for improvements in bagging procedures is

    A. suggestions of employees
    B. recommendations from the auditing department
    C. assistant supervisor's records
    D. the Authority's Rules and Regulations

17.____

18. A railroad clerk working 12:00 midnight to 8:00 A.M. is directed to report to the NYCTA medical staff for a physical examination at 11:00 A.M. of the same day. The pay allowed him for reporting will be _____ hour(s).

    A. 1   B. 2   C. 3   D. 4

18.____

Questions 19-22.

DIRECTIONS: Questions 19 through 22 are based on the situation described below. Consider the facts given in this situation when answering these questions.

SITUATION

John Doe desiring to get to the Stillwell Avenue Station in Coney Island boarded a Manhattan bound train at the Continental Avenue Station in Forest Hills at 11:30 A.M. on a weekday.

19. The total number of lines going to Manhattan from Continental Avenue at this time of day is

    A. 2   B. 3   C. 4   D. 5

19.____

20. A good transfer point where Doe may change trains to reach his destination is

    A. 59th Street and Lexington Avenue
    B. 34th Street and 6th Avenue
    C. 42nd Street and 8th Avenue
    D. Queens Plaza

20.____

21. The train which Doe should board to make the trip in the SHORTEST possible time started from

    A. Continental Avenue
    B. 179th Street
    C. 169th Street
    D. Parsons Blvd.

22. A train he could have transferred to in order to reach his destination without additional change is

    A. IND "A" train
    B. BMT Brighton Express
    C. BMT West End Express
    D. IND "D" train

23. In making a report of an accident on a stairway from the mezzanine to the street at a subway station, the LEAST important of the following items to include is the

    A. time of day
    B. number of steps
    C. date
    D. weather

24. Assume that, when you are inspecting one of your assigned stations, you notice a cleaner who in your opinion is under the influence of liquor.
    Your proper procedure is to

    A. let the porter wait in the change booth and check his condition again later
    B. have the porter escorted to the medical office immediately
    C. have the porter sign out sick and send him home
    D. have the railroad clerk verify your judgment

25. A cleaner brings to you, the station supervisor, a passenger who insists he wants to file a claim against the transit authority.
    Your BEST procedure would be to

    A. have the passenger wait while you call the supervisor for instructions
    B. give the passenger an accident report form to fill out
    C. take down the complaint in writing and tell the passenger he will be contacted by an adjuster
    D. direct the passenger to the transit authority claims department

26. A porter on the day trick, who is called in to work four hours in excess ahead of his regular tour of duty will be allowed for his days work a total of

    A. 8 hours plus commensurate time off
    B. 12 hours
    C. 14 hours
    D. 17 hours

27. When a controversial order is issued, the BEST way for a station supervisor to pass the order on to his men is to

    A. briefly discuss the controversial parts
    B. state that he expects the order to be strictly obeyed
    C. suggest it need not be strictly followed
    D. invite their comments

28. It was recently announced that the Transit Authority will conduct a course in courtesy and passenger relations for all railroad clerks and cleaners in the station department. This course is given MAINLY to

    A. increase subway revenue
    B. assure safety of passengers at all times
    C. improve the quality of service
    D. encourage the public to be more friendly

28.____

29. One of your railroad clerks reporting for work on the 7:00 A.M. trick states that he does not feel well. At 8:15 A.M. he claims he is much worse and requests permission to go home. He refuses to go to the medical office and, as he is obviously sick, you allow him to leave.
The time that should be charged against his sick leave allowance should be _____ day.

    A. one full   B. 3/4   C. 1/2   D. 1/4

29.____

30. Bulletin orders are often reissued without change.
The MAIN reason for doing this is to

    A. make sure that the order gets posted on all bulletin boards
    B. replace any lost copies of the order
    C. remind station employees that the order is still in effect
    D. save time in making up a new order

30.____

KEY (CORRECT ANSWERS)

1.	B	16.	C
2.	B	17.	D
3.	B	18.	C
4.	A	19.	B
5.	D	20.	B
6.	C	21.	B
7.	A	22.	D
8.	C	23.	B
9.	A	24.	B
10.	B	25.	D
11.	B	26.	C
12.	D	27.	A
13.	B	28.	C
14.	B	29.	B
15.	A	30.	C

EXAMINATION SECTION
TEST 1

DIRECTIONS: Each question or incomplete statement is followed by several suggested answers or completions. Select the one that BEST answers the question or completes the Statement. *PRINT THE LETTER OF THE CORRECT ANSWER IN THE SPACE AT THE RIGHT.*

1. A vandal throws a stone and injures a raliroad porter who is working at an elevated train station. When the porter's assistant station supervisor submits a supervisory accident report for the accident to his supervisor for approval, the latter should make sure that the proper category for *RESPONSIBILITY* has been checked off.
   The proper *RESPONSIBILITY* category that should be checked for this accident is

   A. Control of Other Than Company or Employee
   B. Impractical to Control
   C. Supervision
   D. Employee

2. Assume that you are a station supervisor and you notice that the accident rate for a particular heavy duty cleaning gang has increased to an unacceptable level.
   Of the following, the BEST method of handling this problem is to tell the assistant station supervisor in charge of this gang

   A. to watch his men more closely when they work and to correct any unsafe work habits they may have
   B. that the accident rate for his gang is too high and that it reflects poorly on the work record of his gang
   C. that he must severely penalize those men who are most accident prone in order to set an example for the others in the gang
   D. to assign the easiest work tasks to those men who have the most accidents

3. Assume that your superior gives you orders to carry out a special assignment. However, you believe there is an error in his orders.
   Which one of the following statements BEST describes the action you should take in this situation?

   A. Carry out the orders exactly as given to you
   B. Carry out the orders, but modify them to correct the error
   C. Delay carrying out the orders and give your superior a chance to detect the error himself
   D. Point out the error to your superior before carrying out the orders

4. A work sheet for a booth audit has the readings shown below for four turnstiles:

Turnstile No.	Opening Readings	Readings For Audit
1	26178	26291
2	65489	65752
3	72267	72312
4	45965	46199

   With a fare of $2.50, what is the cash value of the total difference between the Opening Readings and the Readings for Audit for the four turnstiles?

69

A. A. $1,587.50   B. $1,632.50   C. $1,637.50   D. $1,687.50

5. When an employee is suspected of being under the influence of alcohol, a member of supervision must make out a written report of the incident. This supervisor should include in his report the answer to certain questions that he has asked the employee. Following are *four* possible questions that the supervisor might ask the employee:
    I. What kind of beverage did you drink?
    II. How much alcohol did the beverage contain?
    III. When did you drink this beverage?
    IV. How much of the beverage did you drink?

    Which *one* of the following choices lists *only* those of the above questions that must be asked for the preparation of the written report?

    A. I, II, and III
    C. I, II, and IV
    B. I, III, and IV
    D. II, III, and IV

5. _____

6. Following are *four* statements relating to collection train operations, which may or may not be correct:
    I. The assistant station supervisor in charge of a collection train must follow the prepared schedule of revenue collections at all times and is not authorized to deviate from it.
    II. The checking of bags delivered to the collection train will be done after the count of bags to the tally clerks has been completed, and while the train is moving from one station to another.
    III. The tally clerk will arrange the railroad clerks' daily reports in booth and trick order, and he will personally deliver these reports to the representative of the revenue department on duty in the revenue room.
    IV. The tally clerk of each revenue train will check keys, dials and related equipment received from collection parties, and will see to the disposition of these items according to scheduled procedure, unless otherwise directed by an authorized supervisor.

    Which of the following choices lists *all* the above statements that are correct and *none* that is incorrect?

    A. I and II
    C. II, III, and IV
    B. I, II, and III
    D. III and IV

6. _____

Questions 7-10.

DIRECTIONS: Questions 7 to 10 require computing basic schedule working time for certain specified tasks for porters assigned to one station. The questions apply to an average station for which the statistics are as follows:

STATION STATISTICS

Tile: 3, 747 linear feet (average height of 9 1/2 feet)

No. of Entrance Stairways: 7

No. of Rolled Platform Columns: Northbound 72,
                                  Southbound 76

Active Floor Area: Northbound Platform 12,345 sq. ft.
                     Southbound Platform 12,987 sq. ft.

7. The total computed time required to sweep all the entrance stairways daily from Monday through Friday is, *most nearly*, _____ hour(s).

   A. 1   B. 4 3/4   C. 5 1/2   D. 6

8. If all the columns in the station must be cleaned once in a period of 4 weeks, the total computed time that should be allotted to the cleaning of columns each week is, *most nearly*, _____ hours.

   A. 6 1/4   B. 7 1/4   C. 8   D. 10 1/4

9. The total weekly computed time for sweeping the active floor area twice a week is, *most nearly*, _____ hours.

   A. 4 1/2   B. 6   C. 8 3/4   D. 9 1/4

10. As a major duty, the tile must be cleaned once in a period of 4 weeks. Therefore, the total computed time for cleaning tile each week is closest to _____ hours.

    A. 18.7   B. 23.4   C. 27.2   D. 93.6

11. Assume that a new procedure affecting railroad clerks is to be put into operation immediately. At a staff conference attended by station supervisors and the chief of operations concerning this new procedure, you had objected to it because you believed it would cause a reduction in efficiency, and you thought the present procedure was adequate. Of the following, the BEST course of action for you to take should be to instruct your subordinates to

    A. follow the new procedure, but indicate to them that you do not like it
    B. follow the procedure which they think is best
    C. avoid following the new procedure until the next scheduled staff conference
    D. follow the new procedure and maintain careful notes on how it works

12. Following are *four* statements relating to procedures for unusual occurrences and the preparation of related reports, which may or may not be correct:
    I. At all times a prompt report of every unusual occurrence should be made by telephone to the field office
    II. The telephone report of the occurrence should include the time, the place, and a concise statement of the circumstances and action taken, including the names and addresses of passengers and the names and badge numbers of employees and police officers involved
    III. If the occurrence is of an emergency nature, the field office should be notified first and the police office and station department office notified afterwards.
    IV. Train whistle signals for help, which consist of one short-one long- one short- one long blast, should be given immediate response by station department employees.

    Which of the following choices lists *all* of the above statements that are correct and *none* that is incorrect?

    A. I and II   B. II   C. III   D. III and IV

13. Following are *four* statements relating to the duties of collecting agents, which may or may not be correct:
    I. A collecting agent may not reveal a safe combination except if he has received a verbal order to do so by the assistant general superintendent or his authorized representative.
    II. Unless specifically excused, each collecting agent while on duty will wear his uniform cap and badge and will also carry his revolver permit on his person.
    III. Revolvers will be issued to collecting agents in the presence of either the transit patrolman or the assistant station supervisor in charge of revenue collections at designated points and returned in the same manner.
    IV. No collecting agent should have his revolver or badge in his possession while off duty.

    Which one of the following choices lists all of the above statements that are correct and *none* that is incorrect?

    A. I and II
    B. II and III
    C. II and IV
    D. III and IV

14. Following are *four* statements relating to time card rules, which may or may not be correct:
    I. The entering of time worked by one employee on another employee's time card is forbidden.
    II. Assistant station supervisors are authorized to make notations on employees' time cards in order to draw the attention of the timekeeper to incorrect entries.
    III. Time cards for court attendance and trial board hearings should be forwarded to the station department office for verification and signature.
    IV. Per annum employees are required to submit their time cards at designated locations on the last day of each bi-weekly pay period.

    Which one of the following choices lists *all* of the above statements that are correct and *none* that is incorrect?

    A. I, II, and III
    B. I, III, and IV
    C. I, II, III, and IV
    D. II, III, and IV

15. As a rule, the stairs at all stations are numbered consecutively beginning at the _____ end.

    A. southeast
    B. southwest
    C. northeast
    D. northwest

16. The type of construction *generally* used for sliding gates at stations is designated as _____ rail.

    A. *E*
    B. *F*
    C. *G*
    D. *H*

17. At 9:00 A.M. you are requested by your superior to investigate a situation which has arisen. Turnstiles at a certain station have been repeatedly vandalized over the past week causing a serious revenue loss to the authority and inconvenience to the public. You are told that this is an urgent job and that you must submit a written report to your superior by 5:00 P.M. of that day.
For the report to be of GREATEST immediate value to your superior, it should contain some of the following items:
    I. A brief statement of the problem
    II. A detailed description of the problem
    III. Detailed plans of the platform and station layout
    IV. An outline of possible practical alternate solutions
    V. Your recommended solution
Which of the following choices lists *only* those of the above items to be included in the report so that the report is of GREATEST immediate value to your superior?

    A. I, III, and IV   B. I, III, and V
    C. I, IV, and V   D. II, III, V

Questions 18-20.

DIRECTIONS: Questions 18 to 20 are based on the article shown below entitled *EMPLOYEE NEEDS*. Refer to this article when answering these questions.

EMPLOYEE NEEDS

The greatest waste in industry and in government may be that of human resources. This waste usually derives not from employees' unwillingness or inability, but from management's ineptness to meet the maintenance and motivational needs of employees. Maintenance needs refer to such needs as providing employees with safe places to work, written work rules, job security, adequate salary, employer sponsored social activities, and with knowledge of their role in the over-all framework of the organization. However, of greatest significance to employees are the motivational needs of job growth, achievement, responsibility and recognition.

Although employee dissatisfaction may stem from either poor maintenance or poor motivation factors, the outward manifestation of the dissatisfaction may be very much alike, i.e. negativism, complaints, deterioration of performance, and so forth. The improvement in the lighting of an employee's work area or raising his level of pay won't do much good if the source of the dissatisfaction is the absence of a meaningful assignment. By the same token, if an employee is dissatisfied with what he considers inequitable pay the introduction of additional challenge in his work may simply make matters worse.

It is relatively easy for an employee to express frustration by complaining about pay, wash room conditions, fringe benefits and so forth; but most people cannot easily express resentment in terms of the more abstract concepts concerning job growth, responsibility, and achievement.

It would be wrong to assume that there is no interaction between maintenance and motivational needs of employees. For example, conditions of high motivation often overshadow poor maintenance conditions. If an organization is in a period of strong growth and expansion, opportunities for job growth, responsibility, recognition and achievement are usually abundant, but the rapid growth may have outrun the upkeep of maintenance factors. In this situation, motivation may be high, but only if employees recognize the poor maintenance conditions as unavoidable and temporary. The subordination of maintenance factors cannot go on indefinitely, even with the highest motivation.

Both maintenance and motivation factors influence the behavior of all employees, but employees are not identical and, furthermore, the needs of any individual do not remain constant. However, a broad distinction can be made between employees who have a basic orientation toward maintenance factors and those with greater sensitivity toward motivation factors.

A highly maintenance-oriented individual, preoccupied with the factors peripheral to his job rather than the job itself, is more concerned with comfort than challenge. He does not get deeply involved with his work but does with the condition of his work area, toilet facilities and his time for going to lunch. By contrast, a strongly motivation-oriented employee is usually relatively indifferent to his surroundings and is caught up in the pursuit of work goals.

Fortunately, there are few people who are either exclusively maintenance-oriented or purely motivation-oriented. The former would be deadwood in an organization, while the latter might trample on those around him in his pursuit to achieve his goals.

18. With respect to employee motivational and maintenance needs, the management policies of an organization which is growing rapidly will probably result

    A. more in meeting motivational needs rather than maintenance needs
    B. more in meeting maintenance needs rather than motivational needs
    C. in meeting both of these needs equally
    D. in increased effort to define the motivational and maintenance needs of its employees

19. In accordance with the above article, which of the following CANNOT be considered as an example of an employee maintenance need for railroad clerks?

    A. Providing more relief periods
    B. Providing fair salary increases at periodic intervals
    C. Increasing job responsibilities
    D. Increasing health insurance benefits

20. Most employees in an organization may be categorized as being interested in

    A. maintenance needs only
    B. motivational needs only
    C. both motivational and maintenance needs
    D. money only, to the exclusion of all other needs

KEY (CORRECT ANSWERS)

1.	A	11.	D
2.	A	12.	B
3.	D	13.	C
4.	C	14.	C
5.	B	15.	A
6.	C	16.	D
7.	B	17.	C
8.	A	18.	A
9.	D	19.	C
10.	B	20.	C

TEST 2

DIRECTIONS: Each question or incomplete statement is followed by several suggested answers or completions. Select the one that BEST answers the question or completes the Statement. *PRINT THE LETTER OF THE CORRECT ANSWER IN THE SPACE AT THE RIGHT.*

1. The following are possible actions that a railroad clerk could take: when a passenger tells him that he lost money in a malfunctioning vending machine:
    I. Close the coin slot on the vending machine
    II. List the name and address of the passenger on the prescribed form
    III. Refund the lost amount of money to the passenger
    IV. Notify the station department control desk

    Which of the following choices lists *all* the correct actions stated above that the railroad clerk should take?

    A. I and II
    B. I, II, and III
    C. I, II, and IV
    D. II and IV

    1.___

2. Assume that 326 railroad porters will begin using a new type of disinfectant at certain stations as part of a test to determine the suitability of the disinfectant for authority use. If 14 ounces of undiluted disinfectant must be added to 3 gallons of water to make a satisfactory solution of the disinfectant and each porter is expected to use approximately 5 gallons of disinfectant solution each week, the amount of undiluted disinfectant needed for *all* the porters for a 6- week test is _____ ounces.

    A. 3890
    B. 4890
    C. 4990
    D. 5890

    2.___

3. Below are *four* possible actions which may or may not be taken in dealing with snow or sleet storms in accordance with standard operating procedures:
    I. Superintendents and station supervisors will communicate with the assistant general superintendent or his designated alternate for any special assignments.
    II. Assistant station supervisors who do not have a telephone at home will be required to communicate with their field office for assignment and if no assignment is given they will report for their next regularly assigned tour of duty.
    III. When a storm is of such severity that assistance from the bureau of track and structures is required, the supervisor on duty in the station department office will make such request to the ranking official of the bureau of track and structures.
    IV. On elevated stations where there are open ties, snow may be thrown between the running rails if extreme care is used to prevent tripping of trains.

    Which of the following choices lists *all* of the above procedures that are correct and *none* that is incorrect?

    A. I and III
    B. II and III
    C. II and IV
    D. III and IV

    3.___

4. If the total number of accidents to the public on authority property in May 2007 was 529 and in May 2008 was 585, the *percent increase* in accidents in May 2008 as compared to May 2007 is closest to

    A. 7%
    B. 9%
    C. 11%
    D. 13%

    4.___

5. You are instructing a newly appointed assistant station supervisor on the procedures for making a semi-annual inspection of a concession on authority property.
You should tell him that if the concession has NO cooking facilities, he should check whether the concessionaire has on his premises a _____ fire extinguisher.

   A. 2 lb. dry chemical
   B. 5 lb. dry chemical
   C. 2 1/2 gallon water-type pressurized
   D. 10 lb. capacity carbon dioxide

5._____

6. The repair of malfunctioning public address speakers in the vicinity of token booths is the responsibility of the

   A. telephone subdivision
   B. station department
   C. rapid transit operations department
   D. signal division

6._____

7. A wooden edging, level with the floor of a concrete platform and running its entire length, which is used to reduce the gap between the platform and a train is called a

   A. rubbing board   B. coping
   C. pantograph   D. slap rail

7._____

8. A railroad clerk, paid $11.48 an hour, works a 7:00 A.M. to 3:00 P.M. tour of duty Monday through Friday.
What is his gross pay for a particular week if he is ordered to instruct a newly-appointed railroad clerk in the performance of his duties in his booth each day of that week during his tour?

   A. $482.16   B. $516.60   C. $533.82   D. $539.56

8._____

9. Assume that your superintendent has asked you to research a problem and to provide him with all the information necessary for him to arrive at a solution. In assembling this information you should be *especially* careful to give him *only* information which

   A. has been collected objectively
   B. will be consistent with previous information on this problem
   C. supports the present thinking of your superintendent
   D. in your judgment will provide the best solution to the problem

9._____

10. The following are possible supervisory practices which a station supervisor might employ to create a healthy climate for work, morale, and discipline among his subordinates:
    I. Tell subordinates that he will not answer questions which are covered by the book of rules
    II. Encourage subordinates to ask questions when in doubt about station department policies
    III. Praise subordinates in public, but reprimand them in private
    IV. Warn subordinates that they should feel guilty about making a mistake
    V. When a mistake is made, immediately institute disciplinary action regardless of the causes
    VI. If a subordinate makes a significant mistake, use the opportunity to teach him the correct procedure

10._____

Which one of the following choices contains *only* those of the above supervisory practices which are helpful for a station supervisor to follow in creating a healthy climate for work, morale, and discipline?

    A. I, II, and IV
    B. I, IV, and V
    C. II, III, and VI
    D. III, IV, and V

11. When formulating the annual operating budget in the station department, it is necessary to determine the number of man-days required to cover the various work programs.
If the railroad porter's work program calls for 2,354 daily tours, 2,163 Saturday tours, and 1,980 Sunday tours (including holidays), then the number of man-days which are normally required to cover this one-year work program without taking into account vacation coverage is, *most nearly,*

    A. 730,000   B. 780,000   C. 830,000   D. 880,000

12. Assume that you are in charge of a field office. At the beginning of your tour on a particular day you are faced with the following *four* almost simultaneous situations:
    I. One of your railroad clerks has telephoned your assistant station supervisor and has asked that you return her call as soon as possible because she has a question about her daily fare report.
    II. One of your railroad porters at an elevated station has telephoned you to report that a small section of one of the concrete platforms has broken off and fallen to the street.
    III. A clerk from the chief of operations office has telephoned you and has requested you to complete and submit to them a special material utilization report immediately, since it is urgently needed at their office.
    IV. One of your assistant station supervisors gives you a written message regarding important information that you must use in the preparation of a statistical report covering emergency actions taken during the preceding month.
Which one of the above four situations should you take care of FIRST?

    A. I   B. II   C. III   D. IV

13. A railroad clerk complains to you that a certain newly appointed assistant station supervisor under your supervision has been making rude and insulting comments to her about her work.
The following are offered as possible actions that you could consider taking in this matter:
    I. Interview the railroad clerk personally and obtain as many details of the alleged incidents as possible
    II. Ask the railroad clerk to be patient with the assistant station supervisor as he is still nervous about his new duties
    III. Tell the railroad clerk to keep a daily log of her encounters with this assistant station supervisor and make a report to you in one week
    IV. Summon the assistant station supervisor and ask him for an explanation
    V. Summon the railroad clerk and explain that this is not your concern but more properly a matter for her union representative
Which of the following choices lists the BEST of the above actions to be taken in handling this matter?

    A. I and II   B. I and IV   C. II and III   D. IV and V

14. You have been assigned to evaluate three different new cleansing powders for tile surfaces and to recommend the use of one of them for the station department. In your investigation you have determined that all of the cleansers can do equally satisfactory jobs. Therefore, your recommendation of the cleanser to use should be based PRIMARILY on which one costs *least* per

    A. pound
    B. square foot of tile cleaned
    C. gallon of water used
    D. package

15. A station supervisor leaves written instructions in connection with a work matter for one of his assistant station supervisors, and, in these instructions, he clearly delegates authority to the latter to supervise the job. In this situation, it would be BEST if the assistant station supervisor

    A. used his delegated authority to make any changes in the scope of the job and its related activities that he feels are necessary
    B. notifies the station supervisor each time he uses his delegated authority on the job
    C. goes to the station supervisor frequently to check out details of the job as it progresses
    D. goes to the station supervisor only if there are unusual problems

16. The station supervisor in charge of a collection train must make sure that the collection train, and, in particular, the car in which the revenue is carried, is NEVER left without *at least* _____ armed guards.

    A. one   B. two   C. three   D. four

17. When a train derailment or other major emergency occurs, the PRIMARY source for information to the news media about details of the incident should be the

    A. director of public information and community relations
    B. executive officer, operations and maintenance
    C. emergency press center
    D. station department office

18. Making supervisory decisions should be based on sound, problem-solving principles. Following are five principles which you might consider in trying to solve difficult problems:
    I. Make sure you understand the problems you are expected to solve
    II. Make sure you have some idea of possible solutions before you start working on the problems
    III. Review the results of past decisions on similar problems to provide helpful precedents
    IV. Consider the possible solutions to the problems without taking into account their consequences
    V. Call on your associates for help, especially those with experience in the areas involved

    Which of the following choices lists *all* of the above principles which are correct and *none* that is incorrect?

    A. I, III, and V   B. I, II, and III
    C. II, IV, and V   D. III, IV, and V

19. *A no clearance area* in the subway is indicated by a sign that has diagonal stripes that are colored *alternately*

   A. red and white
   B. red and black
   C. black and white
   D. black and yellow

20. The operation and maintenance of station department facilities is a continuing process. A station supervisor should seek ways to improve the efficiency of those operations which he supervises by such means as changing established methods and procedures that appear wasteful and inefficient.
   The following are possible courses of action which could be taken when changing established methods and procedures:
   I. Make changes only when your subordinates agree to them
   II. Make changes quickly and quietly in order to avoid dissent
   III. Secure expert guidance before instituting unfamiliar procedures
   IV. Standardize operations which are performed on a continuing basis
   V. Discuss changes with your superintendent before putting them into practice
   Which of the following choices lists *only* those actions stated above which are useful when changing established methods or procedures?

   A. I, II, and III
   B. I, II, II, and V
   C. II, III, and IV
   D. III, IV, and V

21. A location in the subway having a blue light should normally have which of the following types of equipment?
   An emergency alarm box

   A. *only*
   B. *and* a telephone only
   C. *and* a fire extinguisher only
   D. a telephone and a fire extinguisher

22. The train whistle or horn signal which is meant to be an alarm to persons on a station platform consists of _____ blasts.

   A. one long
   B. two long
   C. two short
   D. a succession of short

23. When removing bags of coins from the reserve supply, railroad clerks are directed to place on sale the bag with the

   A. least number of coins
   B. most number of coins
   C. most recent date
   D. oldest date

24. A railroad clerk, paid $10.80 an hour, works a 7:00 A.M. to 3:00 P.M. tour of duty Monday through Friday.
   What is his gross pay for a particular day on which he is required to attend a class on a new station department procedure for two hours after the completion of his tour of duty?

   A. $86.40
   B. $108.00
   C. $118.80
   D. $129.60

25. After using up all time credited to him, a railroad clerk who is eligible to receive 60% sick pay may receive this benefit if he is off sick for a minimum of _____ or more consecutive working days. 25._____

    A. 9   B. 14   C. 21   D. 25

KEY (CORRECT ANSWERS)

1. C		11. C	
2. B		12. B	
3. D		13. B	
4. C		14. B	
5. C		15. D	
6. A		16. B	
7. A		17. C	
8. B		18. A	
9. A		19. A	
10. C		20. D	

21. D
22. D
23. D
24. C
25. A

WORK SCHEDULING

EXAMINATION SECTION
TEST 1

DIRECTIONS: Each question or incomplete statement is followed by several suggested answers or completions. Select the one that BEST answers the question or completes the statement. *PRINT THE LETTER OF THE CORRECT ANSWER IN THE SPACE AT THE RIGHT.*

Questions 1-8.

DIRECTIONS: Questions 1 through 8 are to be answered SOLELY on the basis of the following information and relief schedule. Read the information and look at the relief schedule before you begin answering these questions.

The daily activities of individual Bridge and Tunnel Officers are listed on their relief schedule. Below is the relief schedule of Officer Franklin Pierce for March 20.

OFFICER: Pierce		
TIME	RELIEF SCHEDULE	LANES
6:55 AM - 7:15 AM	Relieves Officer Rodgers	6
7:20 AM - 7:50 AM	Relieves Officer Smith	7
7:55 AM - 8:15 AM	Officer Pierce takes his own relief	
8:20 AM - 8:40 AM	Relieves Officer Jones	4
8:45 AM - 9:15 AM	Relieves Officer Thomas	5
9:20 AM - 10:10 AM	Officer Pierce has tow truck duty	
10:15 AM - 11:05 AM	Officer Pierce takes his own meal	
11:10 AM - 12 Noon	Relieves Officer Rodgers for a meal	6
12:05 PM - 12:35 PM	Relieves Officer James	2
12:40 PM - 1:30 PM	Relieves Officer Jones for a meal	4
1:35 PM - 2:05 PM	Officer Pierce takes his own relief	
2:10 PM - 3:00 PM	Relieves Officer Peterson for a meal	3
3:05 PM - 3:55 PM	Officer Pierce assists the Sergeant	
4:20 PM	Officer Pierce terminates tour of duty	

1. During which one of the following time periods is Officer Pierce scheduled for tow truck duty?

    A. 7:55 AM - 8:15 AM B. 9:20 AM - 10:10 AM
    C. 10:15 AM - 11:05 AM D. 1:35 PM - 2:05 PM

1.____

2. At 12:15 PM, Officer Pierce should be working in lane number

    A. 2   B. 3   C. 4   D. 6

2.____

3. How many times does Officer Pierce relieve other officers for a meal?

    A. 1   B. 2   C. 3   D. 4

3.____

83

4. Officer Jones' meal period begins at 12:40 PM. *At* what time does his meal period end? 4.___
   _____ PM.

   A. 1:30   B. 1:35   C. 1:40   D. 2:05

5. At what time is Officer Pierce scheduled for his own meal? 5.___

   A. 9:20 AM - 10:10 AM   B. 10:15 AM - 11:05 AM
   C. 11:10 AM - 12 Noon   D. 1:35 PM - 2:05 PM

6. Officer Rodgers is relieved by Officer Pierce for a meal. How long is Officer Rodgers' 6.___
   meal period?
   _____ minutes.

   A. 20   B. 30   C. 45   D. 50

7. The assignment which Officer Pierce is scheduled to perform immediately before his own 7.___
   meal time is

   A. tow truck duty
   B. relieving Officer Thomas
   C. assisting the Sergeant
   D. relieving Officer Rodgers for a meal

8. At what time does Officer Pierce's tour of duty end for March 20? 8.___
   _____ PM.

   A. 2:05   B. 3:00   C. 3:55   D. 4:20

Questions 9-18.

DIRECTIONS: Questions 9 through 18 refer to the foreman's time sheet for his crew for one week. The hours worked each day or the reason the man was off on that day are shown on the sheet. *R* means rest day, *A* means annual leave, *S* means sick leave. Where a man worked only part of a day, both the number of hours worked and the number of hours taken off are entered. The reason for absence is entered in parentheses next to the number of hours taken off. These questions are to be answered SOLELY on the information in the time sheet.

Name	Saturday	Sunday	Monday	Tuesday	Wednesday	Thursday	Friday
Smith	R	R	7	7	7	3 4(A)	7
Jones	R	7	7	7	7	7	R
Green	R	R	7	7	S	S	S
White	R	R	7	7	A	7	7
Doe	7	7	7	7	7	R	R
Brown	R	R	A	7	7	7	7
Black	R	R	S	7	7	7	7
Reed	R	R	7	7	7	7	S
Roe	R	R	A	7	7	7	7
Lane	7	R	R	7	7	A	S

9. The caretaker who worked EXACTLY 21 hours during the week is   9._____

   A. Lane   B. Roe   C. Smith   D. White

10. The TOTAL number of hours worked by ALL caretakers during the week is   10._____

    A. 268   B. 276   C. 280   D. 288

11. The two days of the week on which MOST caretakers were off are   11._____

    A. Thursday and Friday   B. Friday and Saturday
    C. Saturday and Sunday   D. Sunday and Monday

12. The day on which three caretakers were off on sick leave is   12._____

    A. Monday   B. Friday   C. Saturday   D. Sunday

13. The two workers who took LEAST time off during the week are   13._____

    A. Doe and Reed   B. Jones and Doe
    C. Reed and Smith   D. Smith and Jones

14. The worker who worked the LEAST number of hours during the week is   14._____

    A. Brown   B. Green   C. Lane   D. Roe

15. The caretakers who did NOT work on Thursday are   15._____

    A. Doe, White, and Smith   B. Green, Doe, and Lane
    C. Green, Doe, and Smith   D. Green, Lane, and Smith

16. The day on which one caretaker worked ONLY three hours is   16._____

    A. Friday   B. Saturday   C. Thursday   D. Wednesday

17. The day on which ALL caretakers worked is   17._____

    A. Friday   B. Thursday   C. Tuesday   D. Wednesday

18. The AVERAGE number of hours per week that each caretaker worked is CLOSEST to   18._____

Questions 19-23.

DIRECTIONS: Questions 19 through 23 are to be answered SOLELY on the basis of the ASSIGNMENT SCHEDULE on the next page. This schedule is similar to one used by Railroad Clerks who have Lunch Relief tours. Railroad Clerks on Lunch Relief tours take over the duties of other Railroad Clerks so that they may go to lunch. In addition, the Lunch Relief Clerk assists, retrieves tokens from turnstiles, sells tokens, watches gates, checks school passes, and escorts other Railroad Clerks from one booth to another. The Lunch Relief Clerks must frequently refer to their schedules.

ASSIGNMENT SCHEDULE

JOB	TOUR	BOOTH HOURS (Mon. - Fri.)	SAT.	SUN.	HOL.
1233	Lunch Relief	7:30 AM - 3:30 PM	9 AM - 5 PM	Same	Same

MONDAY - FRIDAY SCHEDULE

Duties	Station	Booth Number	Time Schedule
Sell Tokens & Assist	Lexington Ave.	N306	7:30 - 9:20
Assist & Escort	42nd - 8th Ave.	N63 to R147	9:30 - 9:40
Lunch Relief	7th Ave. E	N300	9:50 - 10:20
Escort	Lexington Ave.	N306 to N305	10:30 - 10:40
Lunch Relief	59th Street	R158	11:00 - 11:30
Lunch Relief	50th - 7th Ave.	R154	11:40 - 12:10
Lunch Relief	50th - 7th Ave.	R155	12:15 - 12:45
Lunch	Self	-	12:45 - 1:15
Assist & Escort	7th Ave. E	N300 to N301	1:35 - 2:05
Examine School Passes	59th - 7th Ave.	R158	2:25 - 3:30

SATURDAY SCHEDULE

Duties	Station	Booth Number	Time Schedule
Lunch Relief	50th - 8th Ave.	N56	9:00 - 9:30
Lunch Relief	50th - 8th Ave.	N57	9:35 - 10:05
Lunch Relief	50th - 7th Ave.	R154	10:15 - 10:45
Lunch Relief	50th - 7th Ave.	R155	10:50 - 11:20
Assist & Retrieve	42nd - 8th Ave.	N62	11:35 - 1:15
Assist & Retrieve	50th - 8th Ave.	N56	1:25 - 2:30
Lunch	Self	-	2:30 - 3:00
Assist & Sell Tokens	50th - 8th Ave.	N56	3:10 - 5:00

SUN. & HOL. SCHEDULE

Same schedule as Saturday until 11:20 AM, then:

Duties	Station	Booth Number	Time Schedule
Lunch	Self	-	11:20 - 11:50
Assist & Retrieve	42nd - 8th Ave.	N62	12:00 - 12:50
Stand watch over gates	West 4th St.	N80	1:00 - 5:00

19. During which of the following periods does the Railroad Clerk who has Lunch Relief Job 1233 have lunch on Thursdays?

   A. 2:30 - 3:00
   B. 11:00 - 11:30
   C. 11:20 - 11:50
   D. 12:45 - 1:15

20. At which station does the Railroad Clerk who has Lunch Relief Job 1233 act ONLY as an escort?

   A. West 4th Street
   B. 42nd - 8th Ave.
   C. Lexington Ave.
   D. 7th Ave. E

21. Which of the following is one of the holiday duties of the Railroad Clerk who has Lunch Relief Job 1233?

   A. Assist and sell tokens
   B. Assist and retrieve
   C. Lunch relief
   D. Assist and escort

22. At which of the following booths does the Railroad Clerk who has Lunch Relief Job 1233 work on Saturdays? 22._____

    A. N63, N300, N301, N305
    B. N56, N57, N62, N63, N80
    C. N56, N57, N62, R154, R155
    D. N56, N57, N62, R155, R158

23. During which of the following periods does the Railroad Clerk who has Lunch Relief Job 1233 assist and retrieve on Sundays? 23._____

    A. 11:35 - 1:15   B. 12:00 - 12:50
    C. 1:25 - 2:30   D. 3:10 - 5:00

Questions 24-30.

DIRECTIONS: Questions 24 through 30 are to be answered on the basis of the information given in the following SCHEDULED DUTIES of the cleaner assigned to Job 169.

6 (#1)

SCHEDULED DUTIES

JOB 169 8:00 AM	WEST 4TH STREET - A LINE 8:00 AM - 4:00 PM - MONDAY TO FRIDAY ONLY **BOOTH CLOSED SATURDAY AND SUNDAY** Report on duty in uniform to Booth N83 -W. 4th Street
8:00 AM - 8:30 AM	Turn off Post Lights at N83 area. Clean and disinfect crew toilets South end of Northbound lower platform. Fill paper dispensers.
8:30 AM - 11:00 AM	Sweep all street stairways N83 area. Sweep all stairways leading to middle mezzanine. Scrap Northbound upper and lower platforms and North half of middle mezzanine.
11:00 AM - 11:30 AM	LUNCH -- REPORT OUT AND IN AT BOOTH N83
11:30 AM - 2:00 PM	MAJOR DUTIES AT W. 4TH STREET
MONDAY	Sawdust sweep Southbound upper platform and passageways to and including N81 and N83 mezzanine.
TUESDAY	Sawdust sweep Southbound lower platform and all stairways leading to it.
WEDNESDAY	Sawdust sweep 1/2 mezzanine from center to South end.
THURSDAY	Sawdust sweep 1/2 mezzanine from center to North end.
FRIDAY	Sawdust sweep Northbound upper platform and passageways to and including N80 and N83 mezzanine.
2:00 PM - 2:30 PM	Disinfect urine areas behind North end stairways and N81 area.
2:30 PM - 4:00 PM	Rescrap entire area as covered above. Turn on Post Lights before going off duty.
4:00 PM	REPORT OFF DUTY AT BOOTH N83 - W. 4TH STREET

24. The cleaner assigned to Job 169 should turn off the Post Lights between _____ and _____.   24._____

   A. 3:30 PM; 4:00 PM   B. 2:30 PM; 3:00 PM
   C. 8:00 AM; 8:30 AM   D. 10:30 AM; 11:00 AM

25. The cleaner should sawdust sweep half mezzanine from center to North end on   25._____

   A. Mondays   B. Tuesdays
   C. Wednesdays   D. Thursdays

26. The cleaner should sweep all stairways leading to the middle mezzanine in the N83 area between _____ and _____.   26._____

   A. 8:00 AM; 8:30 AM   B. 8:30 AM; 11:00 AM
   C. 11:30 AM; 2:00 PM   D. 2:30 PM; 4:00 PM

27. The cleaner should report off duty at Booth   27._____

   A. N83   B. N81   C. N80   D. S83

28. Each day, the cleaner should clean and disinfect the crew toilets at the _____ end of the _____ platform.   28._____

   A. South; Northbound lower   B. South; Southbound lower
   C. North; Northbound upper   D. South; Northbound upper

29. A MAJOR duty of Job 169 on Friday is to sawdust sweep   29._____

   A. Southbound lower platform
   B. Northbound upper platform
   C. Southbound upper platform
   D. half mezzanine from center to South end

30. Which of the following is a MAJOR duty of Job 169 to be performed between 11:30 AM and 2:00 PM?   30._____

   A. Sweep all stairways in the N83 area
   B. Sawdust sweep all stairways leading to Southbound lower platform
   C. Disinfect urine areas behind North end stairways
   D. Fill paper dispensers in crew toilets

KEY (CORRECT ANSWERS)

1.	B	16.	C
2.	A	17.	C
3.	C	18.	B
4.	A	19.	D
5.	B	20.	C
6.	D	21.	B/C
7.	A	22.	C
8.	D	23.	B
9.	A	24.	C
10.	B	25.	D
11.	C	26.	B
12.	B	27.	A
13.	B	28.	A
14.	B	29.	B
15.	B	30.	B

EXAMINATION SECTION
TEST 1

DIRECTIONS: Each question or incomplete statement is followed by several suggested answers or completions. Select the one that BEST answers the question or completes the statement. *PRINT THE LETTER OF THE CORRECT ANSWER IN THE SPACE AT THE RIGHT.*

1. Assume that a supervisor finds that his employees have become fatigued from doing a very long and repetitious job.
   The one of the following which would be the BEST way to relieve this fatigue is to
   A. assign other work so that the employees can switch to different assignments in the middle of the day
   B. let the employees listen to a radio while they work
   C. break the job down into very small parts so that each employee can concentrate on one simple task
   D. allow the employees to take frequent rest periods

   1.____

2. Assume that one of your subordinates is injured and will be out for at least six weeks.
   Of the following, the BEST way to handle the work normally assigned to this person is to
   A. allow the work to remain uncompleted until the injured person returns, since he is the one who can BEST do this work
   B. divide this work equally among the persons under your supervision who can do this work
   C. do all the work yourself
   D. give the injured person's work to the most efficient member of your staff

   2.____

3. Suppose that another supervisor tells you about a new way to organize some of your unit's work. The idea sounds good to you. However, before you were in this unit, a similar plan was tried and it failed.
   The MOST important thing for you to do FIRST is to
   A. find out why the previous attempt failed
   B. suggest that the other supervisor tell his idea to top management
   C. try the plan to see whether it works
   D. find proof that the plan has worked elsewhere

   3.____

4. One of your subordinates comes to you with a grievance. You discuss it with him so that you may fully understand the problem as he sees it.
   However, since you are uncertain as to the proper answer, you should
   A. tell him that you cannot help him with this problem
   B. tell him that you will have to check further and make an appointment to see him again
   C. send him to see your immediate superior for a solution to the problem
   D. ask him to find out from his co-workers whether this problem has come up before

   4.____

5. A supervisor reprimanded one of his subordinates severely for making a serious error in judgment while performing an assignment for which he had volunteered.
   The supervisor's action was
   A. *incorrect*, chiefly because in the future the worker will probably try to avoid taking on responsibility
   B. *correct*, chiefly because this will insure that the worker will not make the same mistake in the future
   C. *correct*, chiefly because the worker should be discouraged from using his own judgment on the job
   D. *incorrect*, chiefly because the reprimand came too late to correct the error that had already been made

6. Of the following, the BEST way for a supervisor to inform all his subordinates of a change in lunch rules is, in MOST cases, to
   A. call a staff meeting
   B. tell each one individually
   C. issue a memorandum
   D. tell one or two employees to pass the word around

7. For a supervisor to assign work giving only general instructions to his subordinate would be advisable when
   A. the supervisor is confident that the worker knows how to do the job
   B. the assignment is a simple one
   C. the subordinate is himself a supervisory employee
   D. errors in the work will not cause serious delay

8. One of the DISADVANTAGES of setting minimum standards of performance for custodial employees is that
   A. such standards eliminate the basis for evaluating employees
   B. the custodial employees may keep their performance at the minimum level
   C. standards are always subject to change
   D. the supervisor may feel that his initiative is being restricted

9. One of your subordinates has been functioning below his usual level. You feel that something of a personal nature may be affecting his work. When you ask him casually whether anything is wrong, he says everything is fine.
   As a next step, it would be BEST to
   A. make frequent casual and humorous comments about the poor quality of his work but refrain, at this time, from any serious discussion
   B. warn him that failure to maintain his customary level of performance might result in disciplinary action
   C. express your concern privately and reveal your interest in the reason for his change in work performance
   D. discuss with him the work of another employee, suggesting that the other employee would be a good example to follow

10. Assume you are teaching a new job to one of your subordinates. After you have demonstrated the job, you can BEST maintain the worker's interest by
    A. showing him training films about the job
    B. giving him printed material that explains why the job is important
    C. having him observe other workers do the job
    D. letting him attempt to do the job by himself under supervision

11. *Insubordination is sometimes a protest against inferior or arbitrary leadership.*
    For the supervisor, the MOST basic implication of the above statement is:
    A. Accusations of insubordination are easy to make, but usually difficult to prove.
    B. Insubordination cannot be permitted if an organization wishes to remain effective.
    C. When an employee discusses an order instead of carrying it out, he has not understood it.
    D. When an employee questions an order, review it to make sure it is reasonable.

12. In appraising a subordinate's mistakes, a supervisor should ALWAYS consider the
    A. absolute number of mistakes, without regard to severity
    B. number of mistakes in proportion to the number of decisions made
    C. total number of mistakes made by other, regardless of assignment
    D. number of mistakes which were discovered upon higher review

13. If you are the supervisor of an office in which the work frequently involves lifting heavy boxes, you should instruct your staff in the proper method of lifting to avoid injury.
    In giving these instructions, you should stress that a person lifting heavy objects MUST
    A. keep his feet close together
    B. bend at the waist
    C. keep his back as straight as possible
    D. use his back muscles to straighten up

14. Of the following, the BEST qualified supervisor is one who
    A. knows the basic principles and procedures of all the jobs which he supervises
    B. has detailed working knowledge of all aspects of the job he supervises but knows little about principles of supervision
    C. is able to do exceptionally well at least one of the jobs which he supervises and as some knowledge of the others
    D. knows little or nothing about most of the jobs which he supervises but knows the principles of supervision

15. The rate at which an employee will learn will vary according to a number of considerations.
Of the following, which is LEAST likely to be controllable by the supervisor or the trainer? The
   A. manner in which the material is presented
   B. state of readiness of the learner
   C. scheduling of practice sessions
   D. nature of the material

16. When considering whether to use written material rather than oral instructions as a means of giving instructions to employees, the one of the following which should be given GREATEST consideration is the employees'
   A. personal preferences
   B. attitude toward supervision
   C. general educational level
   D. salary level

17. Assume that one of your subordinates has been assigned to attend job training classes.
The one of the following which would probably be the BEST evidence of the success of the course is that the employee
   A. feels that he has learned something
   B. continues to study after the course is over
   C. has had a good class record
   D. improves in his work performance

18. Of the following, the situation LEAST likely to result if a supervisor shows favoritism toward particular employees is
   A. laxity in the work of the favored employees
   B. resentment from the other, less-favored employees
   C. increased ability among the favored employees
   D. lowering of morale among employees

19. The one of the following reasons for evaluating employees' performance, whether done formally or informally, which is NOT considered to be POSITIVE in nature is to
   A. give individual counsel to employees
   B. motivate employees toward improvement
   C. provide recognition of superior service
   D. set penalties for substandard performance

20. Assume that, because there has been an unexpected and temporary increase in the short-term work of your unit, you have had temporarily assigned to you several staff members from another agency.
Of the following, in dealing with these employees, it would be LEAST advisable to
   A. assign them to long-term projects
   B. organize tasks so that they can begin work immediately
   C. set standards, making allowances to give them time to learn your ways
   D. direct them in the same way, in general, as you do your regular staff

5 (#1)

21. It has been suggested that one way to increase employee productivity would be to require employees dealing with the public to have proficiency in a relevant foreign language.
Of the following, the MAJOR reason for implementing such a proposal, from the viewpoint of effective public administration, would be to
    A. encourage the foreign-born to learn English
    B. exchange information more rapidly and accurately
    C. increase the public prestige of the agency
    D. stimulate ethnic pride among all groups

21.____

22. Assume that the clerk who normally keeps your unit's records will be on vacation for four weeks.
If other clerks are equally qualified to keep these records, your BEST choice to replace the clerk would be the person who
    A. has skills which are needed least for other duties during this period
    B. volunteers for this work
    C. is next in turn for a special assignment
    D. has handled this task before

22.____

23. Assume that you have under your supervision several young clerical employees who have the bad habit of fooling around when they should be working.
Of the following, the BEST disciplinary action to take would be to
    A. ignore it; these young people will outgrow it
    B. join in the fun briefly in order to bring it to a quicker end each time it occurs
    C. bring to their attention the fact that this behavior is not acceptable and if it continues shift the make-up of the group to keep these young persons apart
    D. warn them that this type of behavior is reason for dismissal and be quick to make an example of the first one who starts it again

23.____

24. Seeking the advice of community leaders has human relations value for a public agency in planning or executing its programs CHIEFLY because it
    A. allows for the keeping of careful records concerning individual suggestions
    B. lets community leaders know that the agency has regard for their opinions
    C. permits the agency to state in writing which programs seem most appropriate
    D. unifies community leaders against the programs of competing private agencies

24.____

25. Good community relations is often action-oriented.
Which of the following activities of a public agency is LEAST likely to be considered as action-oriented by the people of a local community?
    A. Conducting a survey to gather information about the local community
    B. Extending the use of a facility to those previously excluded
    C. Providing a service that was formerly non-existent
    D. Removing something considered objectionable by the local community

25.____

KEY (CORRECT ANSWERS)

1.	A	11.	D
2.	B	12.	B
3.	A	13.	C
4.	B	14.	A
5.	A	15.	B
6.	C	16.	C
7.	A	17.	D
8.	B	18.	D
9.	C	19.	D
10.	D	20.	A

21. B
22. A
23. C
24. B
25. A

TEST 2

DIRECTIONS: Each question or incomplete statement is followed by several suggested answers or completions. Select the one that BEST answers the question or completes the statement. *PRINT THE LETTER OF THE CORRECT ANSWER IN THE SPACE AT THE RIGHT.*

1. Methods of communication with employees are of three types: oral, written, and visual.
   A MAJOR advantage of the written word is that it
   A. insures that content will remain unchanged no matter how many persons may be involved in its transmission
   B. facilitates two-way communication in delicate or confidential situations
   C. strengthens chain-of-command procedures in transmission of information and instruction by requiring the use of prescribed channels
   D. encourages the active participation of employees in the solution of complicated problems

   1.____

2. The use of the conference technique in training often requires more preparatory work on the part of the trainer than does a good lecture PRIMARILY because
   A. a conference would cover material of a more technical nature
   B. the trainer will be required to supply more printed material to the participants
   C. a conference usually involves a greater number of trainees
   D. the trainer must be prepared for a wide variety of possible occurrences

   2.____

3. The one of the following which is NOT an advantage of the lecture over most other methods of training is that it can be given
   A. over the radio or on record   B. to large numbers of trainees
   C. without interruptions   D. with little preparation

   3.____

4. Of the following, the one which is LEAST appropriate as a purpose for using an employee attitude survey is to
   A. develop a supervisory training program
   B. learn the identity of dissatisfied employees
   C. re-evaluate employee relations policies
   D. re-orient publications designed for employees

   4.____

5. The competent trainer seeks to become knowledgeable both in the work of the agency and in the duties of the positions for which he is to conduct training. Of the following, the GREATEST practical value that result when the trainer gains such knowledge is that
   A. he will be more likely to instruct employees to perform their work in a manner consistent with actual practice
   B. all levels of staff will be favorably impressed by a display of interest in the agency and its work
   C. employees will become familiar with the trainer and will not consider him an outsider
   D. the trainer will gain an accurate picture of the capacity of each employee for training

   5.____

6. Assume that you, the supervisor of a small office, are involved in planning the reorganization of your bureau's work. Management has decided not to inform your staff of the reorganization until the plans are completed.
   If one of your subordinates tells you that he has heard a rumor about reorganization of the department, you should reply that
   A. the reorganization involves the bureau, not the department
   B. you haven't heard anything about departmental reorganization and that he should stop spreading rumors
   C. you will inform your staff at the appropriate time if any definite plans are made involving a reorganization
   D. you do not know what is being planned but will ask your superior for details

7. Of the following training methods, the one in which the trainee's role is usually LEAST active is the _____ method.
   A. case-study   B. conference
   C. group discussion   D. lecture

8. Differences in morale between two work groups can sometimes be attributed to differences in the supervision they receive.
   Of the following, the behavior MOST characteristic of a supervisor of a group with high morale is that he
   A. assigns the least difficult tasks to employees with the most seniority
   B. is concerned primarily with his ultimate responsibility, production
   C. delegates authority and responsibility to his staff
   D. is lenient with his workers when they violate rules

9. Informal performance evaluations of individual employees, prepared systematically and regularly over a period of several years, are considered to be useful to a supervisor PRIMARILY because
   A. he will be able to assign tasks based only on these records
   B. unlike formal records, since they are fitted to the characteristics of individual employees, they provide for quick comparisons
   C. he need not discuss them with employees, since they are informal
   D. whatever personnel action he recommends can be substantiated by cumulative records

10. When instructing first-line supervisors in the proper method of evaluating the performance of probationary employees, it is LEAST important for a higher-level supervisor to
    A. explain in detail the standards to be used
    B. inform them of the possibility of higher management review
    C. caution them concerning common errors of evaluation
    D. mention the purposes of probationary employee evaluation

11. Assume that your agency is considering abolishing its official performance rating system but that you, a supervisor of a fairly large office, would like to devise a system for your own use.
    The FIRST step in setting up a system would be to
    A. decide what factors and personal characteristics are important and should be rated
    B. compare several rating methods to see which would be easiest to use
    C. have a private conference with each employee to discuss his performance
    D. set specific standards of employee performance, allowing your workers to make suggestions

12. The basic organizational structure of a municipal agency may have come about for several reasons.
    Of the following, the MOST important influence on the nature of its structure is the agency's
    A. professional attitude
    B. public reputation
    C. overall goal
    D. staff morale

13. The term *formal organization* refers to that organization structure agreed upon by top management whereas the term *informal organization* refers to the more spontaneous and flexible organizational ties developed by subordinates.
    The one of the following which BEST describes the usual *informal organization* is that it represents a(n)
    A. destructive system of relationships which should be eliminated
    B. concealed system of relationships whose goals are the same as management's
    C. actual system of relationships which should be recognized
    D. dysfunctional system of relationships which should be ignored

14. The reluctance of supervisors to delegate work to subordinates when they should is GENERALLY due to the supervisor's
    A. feelings of insecurity in work situations
    B. need to acquire additional experience
    C. inability to exercise control over his subordinates
    D. lack of technical knowledge

15. Assume that you have just been made the supervisor of a group of people you did not know before.
    For you to talk casually with each of your new subordinates with the purpose of getting to know them personally would be
    A. *advisable*, chiefly because subordinates have more confidence in a supervisor who shows personal interest in them
    B. *inadvisable*, chiefly because subordinates resent having their supervisor ask about their outside interests
    C. *advisable*, chiefly because one of the supervisor's main concerns should be to help his subordinates with their personal problems
    D. *inadvisable*, chiefly because a supervisor should not allow his relations with his subordinates to be influenced by their personalities

16. It has been found that high-producing subdivisions of organizations usually have supervisors whose behavior is employee-centered, whereas low-producing units usually have supervisors whose behavior is work-centered.
Therefore, it could be concluded from these findings that
    A. a high-producing unit may cause a supervisor to be authoritarian
    B. a low-producing unit may cause a supervisor to be work-centered
    C. close supervision usually increases production
    D. employee-centered leadership may reduce production

16.____

17. A recent study in managerial science showed that, as the amount of praise increased and amount of criticism decreased, the supervisor was more likely to be perceived by his subordinates as being
    A. concerned with their career advancement
    B. production oriented, through subtle intimidation
    C. seeking personal satisfaction, irrespective of production
    D. uncertain of the subordinates' reliability

17.____

18. The power to issue directives or instructions to employees is derived from employees as much as from management.
It follows MOST logically from this statement that
    A. attitudes toward management can be changed
    B. emphasis on discipline is needed
    C. authority is dependent upon acceptance
    D. employees should be properly supervised for work to be done

18.____

19. "In the decision-making process, it is a rare problem that has only one possible solution. Such a solution should be suspected of being nothing but a plausible argument for a preconceived idea."
The author of the foregoing quotation apparently does NOT believe that
    A. there is usually only one possible solution to a problem
    B. the risks involved in any solution should be weighed against expected gains
    C. each alternative should be evaluated to determine the effort needed
    D. actions should be based on the urgency of problems

19.____

20. The supervisor who relies on punitive discipline to enforce his authority is putting limits on the potential of his leadership. Fear of punishment may secure obedience, but it destroys initiative. Such a supervisor's autocratic methods have cut off upward communications.
Of the following, the major DISADVANTAGE of such autocratic behavior is that
    A. difficulties in the supervision of his subordinates will arise if limits are placed on the supervisor's responsibility
    B. policies that affect the public will be changed too frequently
    C. the supervisor will apply punishment subjectively rather than objectively
    D. instructions will be obeyed to the letter, regardless of changing circumstances

20.____

21. The need for a supervisor to carefully coordinate and direct the work of his unit increases as the work becomes 21.____
    A. more routine
    B. more specialized
    C. less complex
    D. less technical

22. The MAIN goal of discipline as used by a supervisor should be to 22.____
    A. keep the employees' respect
    B. influence behavior, so that work will be completed properly
    C. encourage the employees to work faster
    D. set an example for others

23. One of your subordinates has exhibited discourtesy and non-cooperation on several occasions. 23.____
    Of the following, the MOST appropriate attitude for you to adopt in dealing with this problem is that
    A. disciplinary measures for such an individual generally creates additional problems
    B. failure to correct such behavior may lead to worse offenses
    C. it is a mistake to make an issue out of minor infractions
    D. the harsher the medicine, the faster the cure

24. Assume that an employee has complained to you, his supervisor, that he cannot concentrate on his work because two of his co-workers make too much noise. You pay particular attention to these employees for several days and do not find them making excessive noise. 24.____
    The NEXT step you should take in handling this grievance is to
    A. have a talk with all three employees, urging them to cooperate and be considerate of one another
    B. arrange for the complainant to change his work location to a place away from the two co-workers
    C. talk to the complainant to find out if the complaint he made to you is the real cause of his dissatisfaction
    D. tell the complainant that you have found his grievance to be unfounded

25. In planning the application of an existing agency program to a local community, it is generally necessary to discover relevant problems and possibilities for service. 25.____
    Of the following, the BEST way to learn about such problems and possibilities for service would usually be to
    A. begin the program on a full-scale basis and await reactions
    B. seek opinions and advice from community residents and leaders
    C. hold staff meetings with agency employees who have worked in similar communities
    D. study official federal reports about already completed programs of the same kind

KEY (CORRECT ANSWERS)

1.	A	11.	A
2.	D	12.	C
3.	D	13.	C
4.	B	14.	A
5.	A	15.	A
6.	C	16.	B
7.	D	17.	A
8.	C	18.	C
9.	D	19.	A
10.	B	20.	D

21. B
22. B
23. B
24. C
25. B

TEST 3

DIRECTIONS: Each question or incomplete statement is followed by several suggested answers or completions. Select the one that BEST answers the question or completes the statement. *PRINT THE LETTER OF THE CORRECT ANSWER IN THE SPACE AT THE RIGHT.*

1. Which of the following characteristics would be LEAST detrimental to a supervisor in his efforts to set up and maintain good relations with other supervisors with whom he must deal in the course of his duties?
   A. Not getting involved in consultation on any supervisory problems they might have
   B. Indicating that they should improve their supervising methods and offering suggestions on how to do so
   C. Emphasizing his own role as a member of management
   D. Sharing information which has proved useful in his unit

1.____

2. Both trainers and supervisors might agree that there is usually a best way to do a particular job. Yet a supervisor or instructor sometimes does not teach a new employee the best way, the most efficient way, to do a complex job. Sometimes, in such cases, the supervisor temporarily changes the sequence of operations, increases the number of steps needed to do a job, or makes other changes in the method, which then deviates from the one considered most efficient.
When is such a difference in approach MOST justified when teaching a new employee a complex job?
   A. When the changes in approach correspond to the learning ability of the new employee
   B. When the new employee's performance on the job is closely supervised to compensate for a change in approach
   C. Where the steps in performing the task have not been defined in a manual of procedures
   D. When the instructor has ideas of improving upon the methods for doing the job

2.____

3. Considerable thought in the field of management is directed toward the advantages and disadvantages of authoritarian methods of influencing behavior, and, in the so-called authoritarian model, a nucleus of rather consistent ideas prevail.
Which of the following is LEAST characteristic of an administrative system based on the authoritarian model?
   A. A conviction of a need for order and efficiency in a world consisting mainly of people who lack direction and incentive
   B. Rules and contracts are the basis for action, and decisions are made on an impersonal basis
   C. The right to give orders and instructions is inherent in the hierarchical arrangement of an organizational structure
   D. Realization that subordinates' needs for affiliation and recognition can contribute to management's objectives

3.____

4. Of the following, the FIRST step in planning an operation is to
   A. obtain relevant information
   B. identify the goal to be achieved
   C. consider possible alternatives
   D. make necessary assignments

5. A supervisor who is extremely busy performing routine tasks is MOST likely making incorrect use of what basis principle of supervision?
   A. Homogeneous Assignment
   B. Span of Control
   C. Work Distribution
   D. Delegation of Authority

6. Controls help supervisors to obtain information from which they can determine whether their staffs are achieving planned goals.
   Which one of the following would be LEAST useful as a control device?
   A. Employee diaries
   B. Organization charts
   C. Periodic inspections
   D. Progress charts

7. A certain employee has difficulty in effectively performing a particular portion of his routine assignments, but his overall productivity is average.
   As a direct supervisor of this individual, your BEST course of action would be to
   A. attempt to develop the investigator's capacity to execute the problematical facets of his assignments
   B. diversify the investigator's work assignments in order to build up his confidence
   C. reassign the investigator to less difficult tasks
   D. request in a private conversation that the investigator improve his work output

8. A supervisor who uses persuasion as a means of supervising a unit would GENERALLY also use which of the following practices to supervise his unit?
   A. Supervises and control the staff with an authoritative attitude to indicate that he is a *take-charge* individual
   B. Make significant changes in the organizational operations so as to improve job efficiency
   C. Remove major communication barriers between himself, subordinates, and management
   D. Supervise everyday operations while being mindful of the problems of his subordinates

9. Whenever a supervisor in charge of a unit delegates a routine task to a capable subordinate, he tells him exactly how to do it.
   This practice is GENERALLY
   A. *desirable*, chiefly because good supervisors should be aware of the traits of their subordinates and delegate responsibilities to them accordingly
   B. *undesirable*, chiefly because only non-routine tasks should be delegated
   C. *desirable*, chiefly because a supervisor should frequently test the willingness of his subordinates to perform ordinary tasks
   D. *undesirable*, chiefly because a capable subordinate should usually be allowed to exercise his own discretion in doing a routine job

10. The one of the following activities through which a supervisor BEST demonstrates leadership ability is by
    A. arranging periodic staff meetings in order to keep his subordinates informed about professional developments in the field of investigation
    B. frequently issuing definite orders and directives which will lessen the need for subordinates to make decisions in handling any investigations assigned to them
    C. devoting the major part of his time to supervising subordinates so as to stimulate continuous improvement
    D. setting aside time for self-development and research so as to improve the investigative techniques and procedures of his unit

11. The following three statements relate to supervision of employees:
    I. The assignment of difficult tasks that offer a challenge is more conducive to good morale than the assignment of easy tasks.
    II. The same general principles of supervision that apply to men are equally applicable to women.
    III. The best restraining program should cover all phases of an employee's work in a general manner.
    Which of the following choices lists ALL of the above statements that are generally CORRECT?
    A. II, III   B. I   C. I, II   D. I, II, III

12. Which of the following examples BEST illustrates the application of the *exception principle* as a supervisory technique? A(n)
    A. complex job is divided among several employees who work simultaneously to complete the whole job in a shorter time
    B. employee is required to complete any task delegated to him to such an extent that nothing is left for the superior who delegated the task except to approve it
    C. superior delegates responsibility to a subordinate but retains authority to make the final decisions
    D. superior delegates all work possible to his subordinates and retains that which requires his personal attention or performance

13. Assume that you are a supervisor. Your immediate superior frequently gives orders to your subordinates without your knowledge.
    Of the following, the MOST direct and effective way for you to handle this problem is to
    A. tell your subordinates to take orders only from you
    B. submit a report to higher authority in which you cite specific instances
    C. discuss it with your immediate superior
    D. find out to what extent you authority and prestige as a supervisor have been affected

14. In an agency which has as its primary purpose the protection of the public against fraudulent business practices, which of the following would GENERALLY be considered an auxiliary or staff rather than a line function?

A. Interviewing victims of frauds and advising them about their legal remedies
B. Daily activities directed toward prevention of fraudulent business practices
C. Keeping records and statistics about business violations reported and corrected
D. Follow-up inspections by investigators after corrective action has been taken

15. A supervisor can MOST effectively reduce the spread of false rumors through the *grapevine* by
    A. identifying and disciplining any subordinate responsible for initiating such rumors
    B. keeping his subordinates informed as much as possible about matters affecting them
    C. denying false rumors which might tend to lower staff morale and productivity
    D. making sure confidential matters are kept secure from access by unauthorized employees

16. A supervisor has tried to learn about the background, education, and family relationships of his subordinates through observation, personal contact, and inspection of their personnel records.
    These supervisory actions are GENERALLY
    A. *inadvisable*, chiefly because they may lead to charges of favoritism
    B. *advisable*, chiefly because they may make him more popular with his subordinates
    C. *inadvisable*, chiefly because his efforts may be regarded as an invasion of privacy
    D. *advisable*, chiefly because the information may enable him to develop better understanding of each of his subordinates

17. In an emergency situation, when action must be taken immediately, it is BEST for the supervisor to give orders in the form of
    A. direct commands, which are brief and precise
    B. requests, so that his subordinate will not become alarmed
    C. suggestions, which offer alternative courses of action
    D. implied directive, so that his subordinates may use their judgment in carrying them out

18. When demonstrating a new and complex procedure to a group of subordinates, it is ESSENTIAL that a supervisor
    A. go slowly and repeat the steps involved at least once
    B. show the employees common errors and the consequences of such errors
    C. go through the process at the usual speed so that the employees can see the rate at which they should work
    D. distribute summaries of the procedure during the demonstration and instruct his subordinates to refer to them afterwards

19. The PRIMARY value of office reports and procedures is to   19.____
    A. assist top management in controlling key agency functions
    B. measure job performance
    C. save time and labor
    D. control the activities and use of time of all staff members

20. Of the following, which is considered to be the GREATEST advantage of the   20.____
    oral report? It
    A. allows for accurate transmission of information from one individual to another
    B. presents an opportunity to discuss or clarify any immediate questions raised by the receiver of the report
    C. requires less office work to maintain records on actions taken when an oral report is involved
    D. takes only a short amount of time to plan and prepare material for an oral report

21. A supervisor who is to make a report about a job he has done can make an   21.____
    oral report of a written report.
    Of the following, which is the BEST time to make an oral report? When
    A. the work covers an emergency situation
    B. a record is needed for the files
    C. the report is channeled to other departments
    D. the report covers additional work he will do

22. Suppose that a new employee has been assigned to you. It is your   22.____
    responsibility to see to it that he understands how to fill out properly the forms he is required to use.
    What would be the BEST way to do this?
    A. Explain the use of each form to the new technician and show him how to fill them out
    B. Give the new employee a copy of each form he must use so that he can learn by studying them
    C. Ask an experienced worker to explain clearly to him how the forms should be filled out
    D. Tell the new employee that filling out forms is simple and he should follow the instructions on each form

23. As a supervisor, you want to have your staff take part in improving work   23.____
    methods.
    Of the following, the BEST way to do this is to
    A. make critical appraisals of their work frequently
    B. encourage them to make suggestions
    C. make no change without their approval
    D. hold regular staff meetings

24. A good relationship with other supervisors is important to a senior supervisor. Close cooperation among supervisory personnel is MOST likely to result in
    A. increasing the probability for support of supervisory actions and decisions
    B. stimulating supervisors to achieve higher status in the organization
    C. helping to control the flow of work within a unit
    D. a clearer definition of the responsibilities of individual supervisors

25. Which of the following is MOST likely to gain a supervisor the respect and cooperation of his staff?
    A. Assigning the most difficult jobs to the experienced staff members
    B. Giving each staff member the same number of assignments
    C. Assigning jobs according to each staff member's ability
    D. Giving each staff member the same types of assignments

KEY (CORRECT ANSWERS)

1.	D	11.	C
2.	A	12.	D
3.	D	13.	C
4.	B	14.	C
5.	D	15.	B
6.	B	16.	D
7.	A	17.	A
8.	D	18.	A
9.	D	19.	A
10.	C	20.	B

21. A
22. A
23. B
24. A
25. C

READING COMPREHENSION
UNDERSTANDING AND INTERPRETING WRITTEN MATERIAL
EXAMINATION SECTION
TEST 1

DIRECTIONS: Each question or Incomplete statement is followed by several suggested answers or completions. Select the one that BEST answers the question or completes the statement. *PRINT THE LETTER OF THE CORRECT ANSWER IN THE SPACE AT THE RIGHT.*

Questions 1-10.

DIRECTIONS: Questions 1 through 10 are to be answered on the basis of the description of an incident given below. Read the description carefully before answering these questions.

DESCRIPTION OF INCIDENT

On Tuesday, October 8, at about 4:00 P.M., bus operator Sam Bell, Badge No. 3871, whose accident record was perfect, was operating his half-filled bus, No. 4392Y, northbound and on schedule along Dean Street. At this time, a male passenger who was apparently intoxicated started to yell and to use loud and profane language. The bus driver told this passenger to be quiet or to get off the bus. The passenger said that he would not be quiet but indicated that he wanted to get off the bus by moving toward the front door exit. When he reached the front of the bus, which at the time was in motion, the intoxicated passenger slapped the bus operator on the back and pulled the steering wheel sharply. This action caused the bus to sideswipe a passenger automobile coming from the opposite direction before the operator could stop the bus. The sideswiped car was a red 2007 Pontiac 2-door convertible, License 6416-KN, driven by Albert Holt. The bus driver kept the doors of his bus closed and blew the horn vigorously. The horn blowing was quickly answered as Sergeant Henry Burns, Badge No. 1208, and Patrolman Joe Cross, Badge No. 24643, happened to be following a few cars behind the bus in police car No. 736. The intoxicated passenger, who gave his name as John Doe, was placed under arrest, and Patrolman Cross took the names of witnesses while Sergeant Burns recorded the necessary vehicular information. Investigation showed that no one was injured in the accident and that the entire damage to the automobile was having its side slightly pushed in.

1. From the information given, it can be reasoned that

    A. it was just beginning to rain
    B. Dean Street is a two-way street
    C. there were mostly women shoppers on the bus
    D. most seats in the bus were filled

2. The name of the policeman who was riding in the police car with the sergeant was

    A. Cross   B. Bell   C. Holt   D. Burns

3. From the description, it is evident that the passenger automobile was traveling   3._____

   A. north   B. south   C. east   D. west

4. It is logical to conclude that the passenger automobile was damaged on its   4._____

   A. front end   B. rear end
   C. right side   D. left side

5. A fact concerning the intoxicated passenger that is clearly stated in the above description is that he   5._____

   A. was intoxicated when he got on the bus
   B. hit a fellow passenger
   C. pulled the steering wheel sharply
   D. was not arrested

6. The bus operator called the attention of the police by   6._____

   A. sideswiping an oncoming car
   B. yelling and using profane language
   C. blowing his horn vigorously
   D. stopping a police car coming from the opposite direction

7. A reasonable conclusion that can be drawn from the above description is that   7._____

   A. the name John Doe was fictitious
   B. the sideswiped automobile was from out of town
   C. some of the passengers on the bus were injured
   D. the bus operator tried to put the intoxicated passenger off the bus

8. The number of the police car involved in the incident was   8._____

   A. 4392Y   B. 6416-KN   C. 1208   D. 736

9. From the facts stated, it is obvious that the bus operator was   9._____

   A. behind schedule
   B. driving too close to the center of the street
   C. discourteous to the intoxicated passenger
   D. a good driver

10. It is clearly stated that the   10._____

    A. sideswiped automobile was a blue sedan
    B. bus driver kept the bus doors closed until the police came
    C. incident happened on a Thursday
    D. police sergeant took down the names of witnesses

Questions 11-20.

DIRECTIONS: Questions 11 through 20 are to be answered on the basis of the paragraph below covering cleaning supplies. Refer to this paragraph when answering these questions.

CLEANING SUPPLIES

Certain amounts of cleaning supplies are used each week at each station of the Transit Authority. The following information applies to a station of average size. For cleaning floors, tiles, and toilets, approximately 14 pounds of soap powder is used each week. A scouring powder is used to clean unusually difficult stains, and approximately 1 1/2 pounds is used in a week. A disinfectant solution is used for cleaning telephone alcoves, toilets, and booth floors, and approximately 1 quart of undiluted disinfectant is used each week. To make a regular strength disinfectant solution, 1/4 ounce of undiluted disinfectant is added to 14 gallons of water. One pint of lemon oil is used each week to polish metal surfaces in booths and in other station areas.

11. In a period of 4 weeks, the amount of soap powder that is used at the average station is MOST NEARLY _____ pounds.

    A. 48   B. 52   C. 56   D. 60

12. In a period of 1 year, the amount of scouring powder that is used at the average station is MOST NEARLY _____ pounds.

    A. 26   B. 52   C. 64   D. 78

13. If a certain large station uses 1 1/2 times the soap powder that an average station uses, then the larger station uses MOST NEARLY _____ pounds a week.

    A. 14   B. 21   C. 24   D. 28

14. To make a regular strength disinfectant solution, the number of ounces of undiluted disinfectant that should be added to 3 gallons of water is

    A. 4   B. 3/4   C. 1   D. 1 1/4

15. To make a double strength disinfectant solution, the number of ounces of undiluted disinfectant that should be added to 3 gallons of water is

    A. 4   B. 3/4   C. 1   D. 1 1/2

16. In a period of 4 weeks, the amount of lemon oil that is used at the average station is _____ gallon(s).

    A. 1/4   B. 4   C. 1   D. 1 1/2

17. In a period of one year, the amount of soap powder that is used at 5 average stations is MOST NEARLY _____ pounds.

    A. 260   B. 728   C. 3,640   D. 5,260

18. To clean a station that is difficult to remove, it would be BEST for a porter to use

    A. soap powder   B. scouring powder
    C. disinfectant solution D. lemon oil

19. Lemon oil should be used for
    A. scouring
    B. regular cleaning
    C. polishing metal surfaces
    D. disinfecting

20. If a smaller than average station uses 3/4 of the amount of scouring powder than an average station uses, then in one week the amount of scouring powder used at the smaller station is MOST NEARLY _____ pound(s).
    A. 7/8   B. 1   C. 1 1/8   D. 1 1/4

Questions 21-25.

DIRECTIONS: Questions 21 through 25, inclusive, are to be answered on the basis of the bus cleaning instructions below, which should be performed in the order given. Read the instructions carefully before answering these questions.

1. SPRAY wheels and mud guards with hand water hose to remove loose dirt.
2. SCRUB mud guards with brush and cleaner.
3. SCRUB wheels with brush and cleaner.
4. SCRAPE grease from wheels with hand scraper.
5. RINSE wheels and mud guards with hand water hose.

21. The cleaning instructions which involve the same parts of the bus are
    A. 1 and 2   B. 1 and 3   C. 2 and 4   D. 1 and 5

22. The scraping takes place
    A. *after* both the spraying and rinsing
    B. *after* the rinsing but before the scrubbing
    C. *before* both the scrubbing and rinsing
    D. *before* the rinsing but after the spraying

23. The hand water hose is NOT used to remove the grease because water
    A. cannot remove the grease properly
    B. would injure the motor
    C. has to be used as cleaner solution
    D. is used only for spraying

24. The brush is used in connection with operations
    A. 1 and 2   B. 2 and 3   C. 3 and 4   D. 4 and 5

25. Loose dirt is removed by
    A. scraping   B. scrubbing   C. spraying   D. rinsing

KEY (CORRECT ANSWERS)

1.	B	11.	C
2.	A	12.	D
3.	B	13.	B
4.	D	14.	A
5.	C	15.	C
6.	C	16.	B
7.	A	17.	C
8.	D	18.	B
9.	D	19.	C
10.	B	20.	C

21. D
22. D
23. A
24. B
25. C

TEST 2

DIRECTIONS: Each question or incomplete statement is followed by several suggested answers or completions. Select the one that BEST answers the question or completes the statement. *PRINT THE LETTER OF THE CORRECT ANSWER IN THE SPACE AT THE RIGHT.*

Questions 1-8.

DIRECTIONS: Questions 1 through 8 are to be answered on the basis of the information contained in the safety rules given. Read these rules carefully before answering these questions.

SAFETY RULES FOR EMPLOYEES WORKING ON TRACKS

Always carry a hand lantern whenever walking a track and walk opposite to the direction of the traffic on that particular track, if possible.

At all times when walking track, take note of and be prepared to use the spaces available for safety, clear of passing trains. Be careful to avoid those positions where clearance is insufficient.

Employees are particularly cautioned with respect to sections of track on which regular operation of passenger trains may at times be abandoned and which are used as lay-up tracks. Such tracks are likely to be used at any and irregular times by special trains such as work trains, lay-up trains, etc. At no time can any section of track be assumed to be definitely out of service, and employees must observe, when on or near tracks, the usual precautions regardless of any assumption as to operating schedules.

1. Safety rules are MOST useful because they

    A. make it unnecessary to think
    B. prevent carelessness
    C. are a guide to avoid common dangers
    D. make the workman responsible for any accident

2. A trackman walking a section of track should walk

    A. to the left of the tracks
    B. to the right of the tracks
    C. in the direction of traffic
    D. opposite to the direction of traffic

3. One precaution a trackman should ALWAYS take is to

    A. have power turned off on those tracks where he is walking
    B. place a red lantern behind him when walking back
    C. wave his lantern constantly when walking track
    D. note nearby safety spaces

4. Special trains are GENERALLY

   A. passenger trains on regular schedule
   B. express trains on local tracks
   C. work trains or lay-up trains
   D. trains going opposite to traffic

4._____

5. A trackman walking track should

   A. stay clear of all safety spaces
   B. expect all trains to be on schedule
   C. avoid tracks used by passenger trains
   D. carry a hand lantern

5._____

6. On sections of track not used for regular passenger trains, a trackman should

   A. follow the rules governing tracks in passenger train operation
   B. assume that no trains will be operating
   C. walk in the direction of traffic
   D. disregard the usual precautions

6._____

7. Safety spaces are provided in the subway for

   A. lay-up trains   B. passing trains
   C. employee's use   D. easier walking

7._____

8. A trackman would NOT expect lay-up tracks to be used by

   A. special trains
   B. trains carrying passengers
   C. work trains
   D. lay-up trains

8._____

Questions 9-17.

DIRECTIONS: Questions 9 through 17 are to be answered on the basis of the porters' instructions given below. Read these instructions carefully before answering these questions

PORTERS' INSTRUCTIONS

Railroad porters are prohibited from entering the token booths except for cleaning or relieving the railroad clerk. When the cleaning or relief has been completed, porters must leave booths immediately and must not loiter in or around the booths. Porters must not leave their equipment or supplies, such as dust pans, brooms, soap, etc., on any stairway, passageway, walkway, or in any place which may result in a hazard to passengers or others. Whenever an accident occurs on the station where the porter is assigned, he must submit a report on the prescribed form, always giving the condition of the place where the accident occurred. Porters must be in prescribed uniforms ready for work when reporting *on* and *off* duty.

9. The instructions would indicate that the porters' PRINCIPAL duty is to

   A. make out accident reports
   B. wear a uniform
   C. relieve the railroad clerk
   D. keep the station clean

10. Porters are permitted to enter token booths

    A. any time they wish
    B. after finishing cleaning
    C. to relieve the railroad clerk
    D. to avoid loitering elsewhere

11. The PROBABLE reason why porters cannot stay in the token booth even if their regular work is done is because

    A. they have a regular porters' room
    B. they are not trusted
    C. there is no room
    D. passengers may complain

12. Porters are used to relieve railroad clerks MAINLY because

    A. they need the training
    B. they are conveniently available
    C. their regular work is hard
    D. their work is similar

13. In submitting a report on an accident, the porter is instructed to

    A. explain the cause
    B. use any convenient paper
    C. give the condition of the place
    D. telephone it to his superior

14. The MOST likely reason for having special uniforms for porters is to

    A. give them authority
    B. avoid a variety of unpresentable clothes
    C. save them money
    D. permit them to enter without paying fare

15. Evidently, porters must be careful where they leave their equipment or supplies to avoid

    A. spoilage   B. theft
    C. loss of time   D. injury to passengers

16. Such instructions to porters are NECESSARY because

    A. there is no other way to do the work
    B. it creates respect for authority
    C. it avoids misunderstandings
    D. they are not expected to think

17. A porter need NOT be in uniform when

    A. doing dirty work
    B. on his day off
    C. reporting *off* duty
    D. relieving the railroad clerk

Questions 18-25.

DIRECTIONS: Questions 18 through 25 are to be answered on the basis of the information contained in the safety rules given below. Read these rules carefully before answering these questions.

TRACKMEN SAFETY RULES ON EMERGENCY ALARM SYSTEM

In case of an emergency requiring the removal of high voltage power from the contact rail, any trackman seeing such emergency shall immediately operate the nearest emergency alarm box, and then immediately use the emergency telephone alongside the box to notify the trainmaster of the nature of the trouble. High voltage will be turned on again only by telephone order from an employee specifically having such authority. The location of this equipment along the trackway is indicated by a blue light. Trackmen are required to know the location of such boxes and the procedure to follow in order to have high voltage contact rail power removed on sections of elevated structure trackway which may not be equipped with emergency alarm boxes.

18. The location of an emergency alarm box is indicated by a(n) _____ light.

    A. red   B. orange   C. green   D. blue

19. Operating an emergency alarm box

    A. calls the fire department
    B. removes power
    C. lights a blue light
    D. restores power

20. All trackmen

    A. have the authority to have power restored
    B. should know the location of emergency alarm boxes
    C. must call the trainmaster before operating an emergency alarm box
    D. do not have the right to operate an emergency alarm box

21. On a track having trains in operation, a nearby emergency alarm box would PROBABLY be operated if

    A. an employee cuts his hand
    B. the emergency telephone rings
    C. the blue light goes on
    D. a break is found in a running track rail

22. After operating an emergency alarm box, the trackman should use the emergency telephone immediately to speak to

    A. his supervisor
    B. the trainmaster
    C. the station agent
    D. his co-workers

23. It would be MOST important to have power restored as quickly as possible in order to reduce

    A. power waste
    B. train damage
    C. train delays
    D. fire hazard

24. If there are no emergency alarm boxes along a trackway, trackmen

    A. cannot have power shut off
    B. are not required to act in an emergency
    C. can have power shut off by following the proper procedure
    D. are forbidden to use the emergency telephone

25. On elevated structure trackways,

    A. emergency alarm boxes may not be found
    B. train delays never occur
    C. the trainmaster is not notified on power removal
    D. power is never removed

KEY (CORRECT ANSWERS)

1. C		11. A	
2. D		12. B	
3. D		13. C	
4. C		14. B	
5. D		15. D	
6. A		16. C	
7. C		17. B	
8. B		18. D	
9. D		19. B	
10. C		20. B	

21. D
22. B
23. C
24. C
25. A

TEST 3

DIRECTIONS: Each question or incomplete statement is followed by several suggested answers or completions. Select the one that BEST answers the question or completes the statement. *PRINT THE LETTER OF THE CORRECT ANSWER IN THE SPACE AT THE RIGHT.*

Questions 1-5.

DIRECTIONS: Questions 1 through 5 are to be answered on the basis of the paragraphs shown below covering the supply duties of assistant station supervisors. Refer to these paragraphs when answering these questions.

SUPPLY DUTIES OF ASSISTANT STATION SUPERVISORS

The assistant station supervisors on the 8 A.M. to 4 P.M. tour will be responsible for the ordering of porter cleaning supplies and will inventory individual stations under their jurisdiction in order to maintain the necessary supplies to insure proper sanitary standards. They will be responsible not only for the ordering of such supplies but will see to it that ordered supplies are distributed as required in accordance with order supply sheets. Assistant station supervisors on the 4 P.M. to 12 Midnight and 12 Midnight to 8 A.M. shift will cooperate with the A.M. station supervisor to properly control supplies.

The 4 P.M. to 12 Midnight assistant station supervisors will be responsible for the ordering and control of all stationery supplies used by railroad clerks in the performance of their duties. They will also see that supplies are kept in a neat and orderly manner. The assistant station supervisors in charge of *Supply Storerooms* will see to it that material so ordered will be given to the porters for delivery to the respective booths. Cooperation of all supervision applies in this instance.

The 12 Midnight to 8 A.M. assistant station supervisors will be responsible for the storing of materials delivered by special work train (sawdust, etc.). They will also see that all revenue bags which are torn, dirty, etc. are picked up and sent to the field office for delivery to the bag room.

Any supplies needed other than those distributed on regular supply days will be requested by submitting a requisition to the supply control desk for emergency delivery.

1. The assistant station supervisors who are responsible for ordering all stationery supplies used by railroad clerks are the ones on the _____ tour.

   A. 8 A.M. to 4 P.M.
   B. 4 P.M. to 12 Midnight
   C. 12 Midnight to 8 A.M.
   D. 4 P.M. to 2 P.M.

   1.____

2. Storing of materials delivered by special work trains is the responsibility of assistant station supervisors on the _____ tour.

   A. 8 A.M. to 4 P.M.
   B. 4 P.M. to 12 Midnight
   C. 12 Midnight to 8 A.M.
   D. 4 P.M. to 2 P.M.

   2.____

3. Torn revenue bags should be picked up and sent FIRST to

   A. the bag room
   B. the supply control desk
   C. a supply storeroom
   D. the field office

4. To obtain an emergency delivery of supplies on a day other than a regular supply day, a requisition should be submitted to the

   A. appropriate zone office
   B. appropriate field office
   C. supply control desk
   D. station supervisor

5. The assistant station supervisor responsible for ordering porter cleaning supplies will inventory individual stations PRIMARILY for the end purpose of

   A. insuring proper sanitary standards
   B. maintaining necessary supplies
   C. keeping track of supplies
   D. distributing supplies fairly

Questions 6-10.

DIRECTIONS: Questions 6 through 10 are to be answered on the basis of the paragraphs shown below entitled POSTING OF DIVERSION OF SERVICE NOTICES. Refer to these paragraphs when answering these questions.

POSTING OF DIVERSION OF SERVICE NOTICES

The following procedures concerning the receiving and posting of service diversion notices will be strictly adhered to:

Assistant station supervisors who receive notices will sign a receipt and return it to the Station Department Office. It will be their responsibility to ensure that all notices are posted at affected stations and a notation made in the transmittal logs. All excess notices will be tied and a notation made thereon, indicating the stations and the date notices were posted, and the name and pass number of the assistant station supervisor posting same. The word *EXCESS* is to be boldly written on bundled notices and the bundle placed in a conspicuous location. When loose notices, without any notations, are discovered in any field office, assistant station supervisor's office, or other Station Department locations, the matter is to be thoroughly investigated to make sure proper distribution has been completed. All stations where a diversion of service exists must be contacted daily by the assistant station supervisor covering that group and hour to ensure that a sufficient number of notices are posted and employees are aware of the situation. In any of the above circumstances, notation is to be made in the supervisory log. Station supervisors will be responsible for making certain all affected stations in their respective groups have notices posted and for making spot checks each day diversions are in effect.

6. An assistant station supervisor who has signed a receipt upon receiving service diversion notices must return the

   A. notice to the Station Department office
   B. receipt to the Station Department office
   C. receipt and the transmittal log to the affected stations
   D. transmittal log after making a notation in it

7. Of the following, the information which is NOT required to be written on a bundle of excess notices is the 7._____

   A. names of the stations where the notices were posted
   B. time of day when the notices were posted
   C. date when the notices were posted
   D. name and pass number of the assistant station supervisor posting the notices

8. If loose notices without notations on them are found, the situation should be investigated to make sure that the 8._____

   A. notices are properly returned to the Station Department
   B. assistant station supervisor responsible for the error is found
   C. notices are correct for the diversion involved
   D. notices have been distributed properly

9. To insure that employees are aware of a diversion in service, an assistant station supervisor covering the group and hour when a diversion exists must contact the involved stations 9._____

   A. immediately after the diversion
   B. on an hourly basis
   C. on a daily basis
   D. as often as possible

10. To make certain affected stations have notices posted when diversions occur, spot checks should be made by 10._____

    A. station supervisors daily
    B. station supervisors when necessary
    C. assistant station supervisors daily
    D. assistant station supervisors when necessary

Questions 11-15.

DIRECTIONS: Questions 11 through 15 are to be answered on the basis of the following paragraph entitled PROCEDURE FOR FLAGGING DISABLED TRAIN.

PROCEDURE FOR FLAGGING DISABLED TRAIN

If at any time it becomes necessary to operate a train from other than the forward cab of the leading car, a qualified Rapid Transit Transportation Department employee must be stationed on the forward end. The motorman and the aforesaid qualified employee must have a clear understanding as to the signals to be used between them as well as to the method of operation. They must know, by actual test, that they have communication between them. Flagging signals should be given at short intervals while train is in motion. If train is carrying passengers, they must be discharged at the next station. Motormen operating from other than the forward cab of the leading car must not advance the controller beyond the *series position*.

11. The qualified employee stationed at the forward end must NOT be a 11._____

    A. motorman   B. conductor
    C. motorman instructor   D. road car inspector

12. While the train is in motion, the employees stationed at the forward end should give a   12.____
    flagging signal

    A. at frequent intervals
    B. every time the train is about to pass a fixed signal
    C. only when he wants the train speed changed
    D. only when he wants to check his understanding with the motorman

13. Motormen operating from other than the leading car must NOT advance the controller   13.____
    beyond

    A. switching   B. series   C. multiple   D. parallel

14. Considering the actual conditions on a passenger train in the subway, the MOST practi-   14.____
    cal method of communication between the motorman and the employee at the forward
    end would be by using the

    A. train public address system   B. buzzer signals
    C. whistle signals   D. lantern signals

15. The BEST reason for discharging passengers at the next station under these conditions   15.____
    is that

    A. carrying passengers would cause additional delays
    B. it is not possible to operate safely
    C. the motorman cannot see the station stop markers
    D. the four lights at the front of the train will be red

Questions 16-25.

DIRECTIONS: Questions 16 through 25, inclusive, are based on the description given in the following special assignment for a group of cleaners. Read the description carefully before answering these questions. Be sure to consider ONLY the information contained in these paragraphs.

SPECIAL ASSIGNMENT

A special assignment of washing the ceilings and the tile walls of a number of stations on a particular line was given to a group of railroad cleaners. The stations included in the assignment were both local and express stations, and the only means of transferring between the uptown and the downtown trains without going to the street was to be found at the express stations. The stations to be cleaned were 2nd Street, 9th Street, 16th Street, 22nd Street, 29th Street, 36th Street, 44th Street, 52nd Street, 60th Street, and 69th Street. Of these, the express stations were located at 16th Street, 44th Street, and 69th Street.

Only the uptown sides of the stations were to be cleaned, as another gang was to clean the downtown sides. The cleaning operations were to start at 2nd Street and progress uptown. The materials furnished to perform this work consisted of pails, soap, long-handled brushes, mops, rags, and canvas covers for scales and vending machines.

The instructions were to scrub a surface first with a brush that had been immersed in a pail of soapy water, and then follow up by brushing with clear water. Any equipment on stations that was left uncovered and was splashed in the cleaning process was to be wiped clean with a rag.

16. The total number of different kinds of materials furnished to do the work of the special assignment was   16.____

    A. 5   B. 6   C. 7   D. 8

17. Benches on station platforms were to be   17.____

    A. moved out of the work area
    B. covered with canvas
    C. wiped clean with a rag if splashed
    D. rinsed with clear water

18. Of the materials furnished, the instructions did NOT definitely call for the use of   18.____

    A. mops   B. brushes   C. pails   D. rags

19. The FIRST operation cleaners were instructed to do was to   19.____

    A. clean walls with scouring cleanser
    B. scrub ceilings with clear water
    C. wipe vending machines clean with rags
    D. scrub surfaces with soapy water

20. Furnished materials that were NOT used in the washing of ceilings included   20.____

    A. soap   B. pails   C. rags   D. water

21. Long-handled brushes were probably furnished because   21.____

    A. ladders cannot be used on stations
    B. such brushes are easier to handle than ordinary brushes
    C. a better job can be done, since both hands are used
    D. some areas could not be reached otherwise

22. Of the total number of stations included in the assignment, the number which were express stations was   22.____

    A. 3   B. 7   C. 10   D. 20

23. A cleaner working in the *uptown* gang at 52nd Street Station was sent by his supervisor to get some supplies from the *downtown* gang which happened to be working at the same station.   23.____
    The cleaner would have displayed good judgment if he

    A. boarded a downtown train to 44th Street, crossed over, and then boarded an uptown train
    B. descended to the tracks and crossed over cautiously
    C. boarded an uptown train to 69th Street, crossed over, and then boarded a downtown train
    D. went directly up to the street and crossed over

24. After finishing the assigned work at 44th Street, the men on this assignment were scheduled to go next to _____ Street.

    A. 16th   B. 36th   C. 52nd   D. 69th

25. A passenger at 29th Street wishing to transfer from a downtown local to an uptown local without paying an additional fare should transfer at _____ Street.

    A. 44th   B. 16th   C. 36th   D. 22nd

KEY (CORRECT ANSWERS)

1. B
2. C
3. D
4. C
5. A

6. B
7. B
8. D
9. C
10. A

11. D
12. A
13. B
14. B
15. A

16. B
17. C
18. A
19. D
20. C

21. D
22. A
23. D
24. C
25. B

PHILOSOPHY, PRINCIPLES, PRACTICES, AND TECHNICS OF SUPERVISION, ADMINISTRATION, MANAGEMENT, AND ORGANIZATION

TABLE OF CONTENTS

	Page
MEANING OF SUPERVISION	1
THE OLD AND THE NEW SUPERVISION	1
THE EIGHT (8) BASIC PRINCIPLES OF THE NEW SUPERVISION	1
I. Principle of Responsibility	1
II. Principle of Authority	2
III. Principle of Self-Growth	2
IV. Principle of Individual Worth	2
V. Principle of Creative Leadership	2
VI. Principle of Success and Failure	2
VII. Principle of Science	3
VIII. Principle of Cooperation	3
WHAT IS ADMINISTRATION?	3
I. Practices Commonly Classed as "Supervisory"	3
II. Practices Commonly Classed as "Administrative"	3
III. Practices Commonly Classed as Both "Supervisory" and "Administrative"	4
RESPONSIBILITIES OF THE SUPERVISOR	4
COMPETENCIES OF THE SUPERVISOR	4
THE PROFESSIONAL SUPERVISOR-EMPLOYEE RELATIONSHIP	4
MINI-TEXT IN SUPERVISION, ADMINISTRATION, MANAGEMENT, AND ORGANIZATION	5
I. Brief Highlights	5
A. Levels of Management	6
B. What the Supervisor Must Learn	6
C. A Definition of Supervision	6
D. Elements of the Team Concept	6
E. Principles of Organization	6
F. The Four Important Parts of Every Job	7
G. Principles of Delegation	7
H. Principles of Effective Communications	7
I. Principles of Work Improvement	7
J. Areas of Job Improvement	7
K. Seven Key Points in Making Improvements	8

	L.	Corrective Techniques for Job Improvement	8
	M.	A Planning Checklist	8
	N.	Five Characteristics of Good Directions	9
	O.	Types of Directions	9
	P.	Controls	9
	Q.	Orienting the New Employee	9
	R.	Checklist for Orienting New Employees	9
	S.	Principles of Learning	10
	T.	Causes of Poor Performance	10
	U.	Four Major Steps in On-the-Job Instructions	10
	V.	Employees Want Five Things	10
	W.	Some Don'ts in Regard to Praise	11
	X.	How to Gain Your Workers' Confidence	11
	Y.	Sources of Employee Problems	11
	Z.	The Supervisor's Key to Discipline	11
	AA.	Five Important Processes of Management	12
	BB.	When the Supervisor Fails to Plan	12
	CC.	Fourteen General Principles of Management	12
	DD.	Change	12
II.	Brief Topical Summaries		13
	A.	Who/What is the Supervisor?	13
	B.	The Sociology of Work	13
	C.	Principles and Practices of Supervision	14
	D.	Dynamic Leadership	14
	E.	Processes for Solving Problems	15
	F.	Training for Results	15
	G.	Health, Safety, and Accident Prevention	16
	H.	Equal Employment Opportunity	16
	I.	Improving Communications	16
	J.	Self-Development	17
	K.	Teaching and Training	17
		1. The Teaching Process	17
		a. Preparation	17
		b. Presentation	18
		c. Summary	18
		d. Application	18
		e. Evaluation	18
		2. Teaching Methods	18
		a. Lecture	18
		b. Discussion	18
		c. Demonstration	19
		d. Performance	19
		e. Which Method to Use	19

PHILOSOPHY, PRINCIPLES, PRACTICES, AND TECHNICS OF SUPERVISION, ADMINISTRATION, MANAGEMENT, AND ORGANIZATION

MEANING OF SUPERVISION

The extension of the democratic philosophy has been accompanied by an extension in the scope of supervision. Modern leaders and supervisors no longer think of supervision in the narrow sense of being confined chiefly to visiting employees, supplying materials, or rating the staff. They regard supervision as being intimately related to all the concerned agencies of society, they speak of the supervisor's function in terms of "growth," rather than the "improvement" of employees.

This modern concept of supervision may be defined as follows: Supervision is leadership and the development of leadership within groups which are cooperatively engaged in inspection, research, training, guidance, and evaluation.

THE OLD AND THE NEW SUPERVISION

TRADITIONAL
1. Inspection
2. Focused on the employee
3. Visitation
4. Random and haphazard
5. Imposed and authoritarian
6. One person usually

MODERN
1. Study and analysis
2. Focused on aims, materials, methods, supervisors, employees, environment
3. Demonstrations, intervisitation, workshops, directed reading, bulletins, etc.
4. Definitely organized and planned (scientific)
5. Cooperative and democratic
6. Many persons involved (creative)

THE EIGHT (8) BASIC PRINCIPLES OF THE NEW SUPERVISION

I. Principle of Responsibility
   Authority to act and responsibility for acting must be joined.
   A. If you give responsibility, give authority.
   B. Define employee duties clearly.
   C. Protect employees from criticism by others.
   D. Recognize the rights as well as obligations of employees.
   E. Achieve the aims of a democratic society insofar as it is possible within the area of your work.
   F. Establish a situation favorable to training and learning.
   G. Accept ultimate responsibility for everything done in your section, unit, office, division, department.
   H. Good administration and good supervision are inseparable.

II. Principle of Authority
The success of the supervisor is measured by the extent to which the power of authority is not used.
- A. Exercise simplicity and informality in supervision
- B. Use the simplest machinery of supervision
- C. If it is good for the organization as a whole, it is probably justified.
- D. Seldom be arbitrary or authoritative.
- E. Do not base your work on the power of position or of personality.
- F. Permit and encourage the free expression of opinions.

III. Principle of Self-Growth
The success of the supervisor is measured by the extent to which, and the speed with which, he is no longer needed.
- A. Base criticism on principles, not on specifics.
- B. Point out higher activities to employees.
- C. Train for self-thinking by employees to meet new situations.
- D. Stimulate initiative, self-reliance, and individual responsibility
- E. Concentrate on stimulating the growth of employees rather than on removing defects.

IV. Principle of Individual Worth
Respect for the individual is a paramount consideration in supervision.
- A. Be human and sympathetic in dealing with employees.
- B. Don't nag about things to be done.
- C. Recognize the individual differences among employees and seek opportunities to permit best expression of each personality.

V. Principle of Creative Leadership
The best supervision is that which is not apparent to the employee.
- A. Stimulate, don't drive employees to creative action.
- B. Emphasize doing good things.
- C. Encourage employees to do what they do best.
- D. Do not be too greatly concerned with details of subject or method.
- E. Do not be concerned exclusively with immediate problems and activities.
- F. Reveal higher activities and make them both desired and maximally possible.
- G. Determine procedures in the light of each situation but see that these are derived from a sound basic philosophy.
- H. Aid, inspire, and lead so as to liberate the creative spirit latent in all good employees.

VI. Principle of Success and Failure
There are no unsuccessful employees, only unsuccessful supervisors who have failed to give proper leadership.
- A. Adapt suggestions to the capacities, attitudes, and prejudices of employees.
- B. Be gradual, be progressive, be persistent.
- C. Help the employee find the general principle; have the employee apply his own problem to the general principle.
- D. Give adequate appreciation for good work and honest effort.
- E. Anticipate employee difficulties and help to prevent them.
- F. Encourage employees to do the desirable things they will do anyway.
- G. Judge your supervision by the results it secures.

VII. Principle of Science
Successful supervision is scientific, objective, and experimental. It is based on facts, not on prejudices.
- A. Be cumulative in results.
- B. Never divorce your suggestions from the goals of training.
- C. Don't be impatient of results.
- D. Keep all matters on a professional, not a personal, level.
- E. Do not be concerned exclusively with immediate problems and activities.
- F. Use objective means of determining achievement and rating where possible.

VIII. Principle of Cooperation
Supervision is a cooperative enterprise between supervisor and employee.
- A. Begin with conditions as they are.
- B. Ask opinions of all involved when formulating policies.
- C. Organization is as good as its weakest link.
- D. Let employees help to determine policies and department programs.
- E. Be approachable and accessible—physically and mentally.
- F. Develop pleasant social relationships.

WHAT IS ADMINISTRATION

Administration is concerned with providing the environment, the material facilities, and the operational procedures that will promote the maximum growth and development of supervisors and employees. (Organization is an aspect and a concomitant of administration.)

There is no sharp line of demarcation between supervision and administration; these functions are intimately interrelated and, often, overlapping. They are complementary activities.

I. Practices Commonly Classed as "Supervisory"
- A. Conducting employees' conferences
- B. Visiting sections, units, offices, divisions, departments
- C. Arranging for demonstrations
- D. Examining plans
- E. Suggesting professional reading
- F. Interpreting bulletins
- G. Recommending in-service training courses
- H. Encouraging experimentation
- I. Appraising employee morale
- J. Providing for intervisitation

II. Practices Commonly Classified as "Administrative"
- A. Management of the office
- B. Arrangement of schedules for extra duties
- C. Assignment of rooms or areas
- D. Distribution of supplies
- E. Keeping records and reports
- F. Care of audio-visual materials
- G. Keeping inventory records
- H. Checking record cards and books

I. Programming special activities
J. Checking on the attendance and punctuality of employees

III. Practices Commonly Classified as Both "Supervisory" and "Administrative"
   A. Program construction
   B. Testing or evaluating outcomes
   C. Personnel accounting
   D. Ordering instructional materials

RESPONSIBILITIES OF THE SUPERVISOR

A person employed in a supervisory capacity must constantly be able to improve his own efficiency and ability. He represent the employer to the employees and only continuous self-examination can make him a capable supervisor.

Leadership and training are the supervisor's responsibility. An efficient working unit is one in which the employees work with the supervisor. It is his job to bring out the best in his employees. He must always be relaxed, courteous, and calm in his association with his employees. Their feelings are important, and a harsh attitude does not develop the most efficient employees.

COMPETENCES OF THE SUPERVISOR

I. Complete knowledge of the duties and responsibilities of his position.
II. To be able to organize a job, plan ahead, and carry through.
III. To have self-confidence and initiative.
IV. To be able to handle the unexpected situation and make quick decisions.
V. To be able to properly train subordinates in the positions they are best suited for.
VI. To be able to keep good human relations among his subordinates.
VII. To be able to keep good human relations between his subordinates and himself and to earn their respect and trust.

THE PROFESSIONAL SUPERVISOR-EMPLOYEE RELATIONSHIP

There are two kinds of efficiency: one kind is only apparent and is produced in organizations through the exercise of mere discipline; this is but a simulation of the second, or true, efficiency which springs from spontaneous cooperation. If you are a manager, no matter how great or small your responsibility, it is your job, in the final analysis, to create and develop this involuntary cooperation among the people whom you supervise. For, no matter how powerful a combination of money, machines, and materials a company may have, this is a dead and sterile thing without a team of willing, thinking, and articulate people to guide it.

The following 21 points are presented as indicative of the exemplary basic relationship that should exist between supervisor and employee:

1. Each person wants to be liked and respected by his fellow employee and wants to be treated with consideration and respect by his superior.
2. The most competent employee will make an error. However, in a unit where good relations exist between the supervisor and his employees, tenseness and fear do not exist. Thus, errors are not hidden or covered up, and the efficiency of a unit is not impaired.

3. Subordinates resent rules, regulations, or orders that are unreasonable or unexplained.
4. Subordinates are quick to resent unfairness, harshness, injustices, and favoritism.
5. An employee will accept responsibility if he knows that he will be complimented for a job well done, and not too harshly chastised for failure; that his supervisor will check the cause of the failure, and, if it was the supervisor's fault, he will assume the blame therefore. If it was the employee's fault, his supervisor will explain the correct method or means of handling the responsibility.
6. An employee wants to receive credit for a suggestion he has made, that is used. If a suggestion cannot be used, the employee is entitled to an explanation. The supervisor should not say "no" and close the subject.
7. Fear and worry slow up a worker's ability. Poor working environment can impair his physical and mental health. A good supervisor avoids forceful methods, threats, and arguments to get a job done.
8. A forceful supervisor is able to train his employees individually and as a team, and is able to motivate them in the proper channels.
9. A mature supervisor is able to properly evaluate his subordinates and to keep them happy and satisfied.
10. A sensitive supervisor will never patronize his subordinates.
11. A worthy supervisor will respect his employees' confidences.
12. Definite and clear-cut responsibilities should be assigned to each executive.
13. Responsibility should always be coupled with corresponding authority.
14. No change should be made in the scope or responsibilities of a position without a definite understanding to that effect on the part of all persons concerned.
15. No executive or employee, occupying a single position in the organization, should be subject to definite orders from more than one source.
16. Orders should never be given to subordinates over the head of a responsible executive. Rather than do this, the officer in question should be supplanted.
17. Criticisms of subordinates should, whoever possible, be made privately, and in no case should a subordinate be criticized in the presence of executives or employees of equal or lower rank.
18. No dispute or difference between executives or employees as to authority or responsibilities should be considered too trivial for prompt and careful adjudication.
19. Promotions, wage changes, and disciplinary action should always be approved by the executive immediately superior to the one directly responsible.
20. No executive or employee should ever be required, or expected, to be at the same time an assistant to, and critic of, another.
21. Any executive whose work is subject to regular inspection should, wherever practicable, be given the assistance and facilities necessary to enable him to maintain an independent check of the quality of his work.

MINI-TEXT IN SUPERVISION, ADMINISTRATION, MANAGEMENT, AND ORGANIZATION

I. Brief Highlights

Listed concisely and sequentially are major headings and important data in the field for quick recall and review.

A. Levels of Management
Any organization of some size has several levels of management. In terms of a ladder, the levels are:

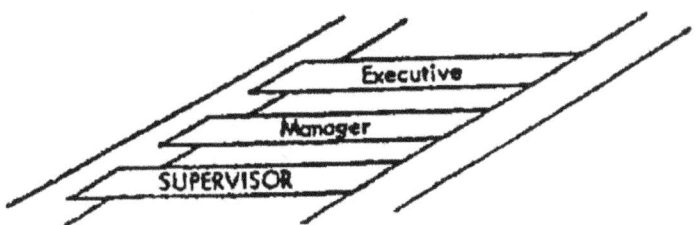

The first level is very important because it is the beginning point of management leadership.

B. What the Supervisor Must Learn
A supervisor must learn to:
1. Deal with people and their differences
2. Get the job done through people
3. Recognize the problems when they exist
4. Overcome obstacles to good performance
5. Evaluate the performance of people
6. Check his own performance in terms of accomplishment

C. A Definition of Supervisor
The term supervisor means any individual having authority, in the interests of the employer, to hire, transfer, suspend, lay-off, recall, promote, discharge, assign, reward, or discipline other employees or responsibility to direct them, or to adjust their grievances, or effectively to recommend such action, if, in connection with the foregoing, exercise of such authority is not of a merely routine or clerical nature but requires the use of independent judgment.

D. Elements of the Team Concept
What is involved in teamwork? The component parts are:
1. Members
2. A leader
3. Goals
4. Plans
5. Cooperation
6. Spirit

E. Principles of Organization
1. A team member must know what his job is.
2. Be sure that the nature and scope of a job are understood.
3. Authority and responsibility should be carefully spelled out.
4. A supervisor should be permitted to make the maximum number of decisions affecting his employees.
5. Employees should report to only one supervisor.
6. A supervisor should direct only as many employees as he can handle effectively.
7. An organization plan should be flexible.

8. Inspection and performance of work should be separate.
9. Organizational problems should receive immediate attention.
10. Assign work in line with ability and experience.

F. The Four Important Parts of Every Job
1. Inherent in every job is the *accountability* for results.
2. A second set of factors in every job is *responsibilities*.
3. Along with duties and responsibilities one must have the *authority* to act within certain limits without obtaining permission to proceed.
4. No job exists in a vacuum. The supervisor is surrounded by key *relationships*.

G. Principles of Delegation
Where work is delegated for the first time, the supervisor should think in terms of these questions:
1. Who is best qualified to do this?
2. Can an employee improve his abilities by doing this?
3. How long should an employee spend on this?
4. Are there any special problems for which he will need guidance?
5. How broad a delegation can I make?

H. Principles of Effective Communications
1. Determine the media.
2. To whom directed?
3. Identification and source authority.
4. Is communication understood?

I. Principles of Work Improvement
1. Most people usually do only the work which is assigned to them.
2. Workers are likely to fit assigned work into the time available to perform it.
3. A good workload usually stimulates output.
4. People usually do their best work when they know that results will be reviewed or inspected.
5. Employees usually feel that someone else is responsible for conditions of work, workplace layout, job methods, type of tools/equipment, and other such factors.
6. Employees are usually defensive about their job security.
7. Employees have natural resistance to change.
8. Employees can support or destroy a supervisor.
9. A supervisor usually earns the respect of his people through his personal example of diligence and efficiency.

J. Areas of Job Improvement
The areas of job improvement are quite numerous, but the most common ones which a supervisor can identify and utilize are:
1. Departmental layout
2. Flow of work
3. Workplace layout
4. Utilization of manpower
5. Work methods
6. Materials handling

7. Utilization
8. Motion economy

K. Seven Key Points in Making Improvements
1. Select the job to be improved
2. Study how it is being done now
3. Question the present method
4. Determine actions to be taken
5. Chart proposed method
6. Get approval and apply
7. Solicit worker participation

L. Corrective Techniques of Job Improvement
Specific Problems
1. Size of workload
2. Inability to meet schedules
3. Strain and fatigue
4. Improper use of men and skills
5. Waste, poor quality, unsafe conditions
6. Bottleneck conditions that hinder output
7. Poor utilization of equipment and machine
8. Efficiency and productivity of labor

General Improvement
1. Departmental layout
2. Flow of work
3. Work plan layout
4. Utilization of manpower
5. Work methods
6. Materials handling
7. Utilization of equipment
8. Motion economy

Corrective Techniques
1. Study with scale model
2. Flow chart study
3. Motion analysis
4. Comparison of units produced to standard allowance
5. Methods analysis
6. Flow chart and equipment study
7. Down time vs. running time
8. Motion analysis

M. A Planning Checklist
1. Objectives
2. Controls
3. Delegations
4. Communications
5. Resources
6. Manpower

7. Equipment
8. Supplies and materials
9. Utilization of time
10. Safety
11. Money
12. Work
13. Timing of improvements

N. Five Characteristics of Good Directions
In order to get results, directions must be:
1. Possible of accomplishment
2. Agreeable with worker interests
3. Related to mission
4. Planned and complete
5. Unmistakably clear

O. Types of Directions
1. Demands or direct orders
2. Requests
3. Suggestion or implication
4. volunteering

P. Controls
A typical listing of the overall areas in which the supervisor should establish controls might be:
1. Manpower
2. Materials
3. Quality of work
4. Quantity of work
5. Time
6. Space
7. Money
8. Methods

Q. Orienting the New Employee
1. Prepare for him
2. Welcome the new employee
3. Orientation for the job
4. Follow-up

R. Checklist for Orienting New Employees   Yes   No
1. Do you appreciate the feelings of new employees
   when they first report for work?   ___   ___
2. Are you aware of the fact that the new employee must
   make a big adjustment to his job?   ___   ___
3. Have you given him good reasons for liking the job and
   the organization?   ___   ___
4. Have you prepared for his first day on the job?   ___   ___
5. Did you welcome him cordially and make him feel needed?   ___   ___

	Yes	No

6. Did you establish rapport with him so that he feels free to talk and discuss matters with you? ___ ___
7. Did you explain his job to him and his relationship to you? ___ ___
8. Does he know that his work will be evaluated periodically on a basis that is fair and objective? ___ ___
9. Did you introduce him to his fellow workers in such a way that they are likely to accept him? ___ ___
10. Does he know what employee benefits he will receive? ___ ___
11. Does he understand the importance of being on the job and what to do if he must leave his duty station? ___ ___
12. Has he been impressed with the importance of accident prevention and safe practice? ___ ___
13. Does he generally know his way around the department? ___ ___
14. Is he under the guidance of a sponsor who will teach the right way of doing things? ___ ___
15. Do you plan to follow-up so that he will continue to adjust successfully to his job? ___ ___

S. Principles of Learning
 1. Motivation
 2. Demonstration or explanation
 3. Practice

T. Causes of Poor Performance
 1. Improper training for job
 2. Wrong tools
 3. Inadequate directions
 4. Lack of supervisory follow-up
 5. Poor communications
 6. Lack of standards of performance
 7. Wrong work habits
 8. Low morale
 9. Other

U. Four Major Steps in On-The-Job Instruction
 1. Prepare the worker
 2. Present the operation
 3. Tryout performance
 4. Follow-up

V. Employees Want Five Things
 1. Security
 2. Opportunity
 3. Recognition
 4. Inclusion
 5. Expression

W. Some Don'ts in Regard to Praise
1. Don't praise a person for something he hasn't done.
2. Don't praise a person unless you can be sincere.
3. Don't be sparing in praise just because your superior withholds it from you.
4. Don't let too much time elapse between good performance and recognition of it

X. How to Gain Your Workers' Confidence
Methods of developing confidence include such things as:
1. Knowing the interests, habits, hobbies of employees
2. Admitting your own inadequacies
3. Sharing and telling of confidence in others
4. Supporting people when they are in trouble
5. Delegating matters that can be well handled
6. Being frank and straightforward about problems and working conditions
7. Encouraging others to bring their problems to you
8. Taking action on problems which impede worker progress

Y. Sources of Employee Problems
On-the-job causes might be such things as:
1. A feeling that favoritism is exercised in assignments
2. Assignment of overtime
3. An undue amount of supervision
4. Changing methods or systems
5. Stealing of ideas or trade secrets
6. Lack of interest in job
7. Threat of reduction in force
8. Ignorance or lack of communications
9. Poor equipment
10. Lack of knowing how supervisor feels toward employee
11. Shift assignments

Off-the-job problems might have to do with:
1. Health
2. Finances
3. Housing
4. Family

Z. The Supervisor's Key to Discipline
There are several key points about discipline which the supervisor should keep in mind:
1. Job discipline is one of the disciplines of life and is directed by the supervisor.
2. It is more important to correct an employee fault than to fix blame for it.
3. Employee performance is affected by problems both on the job and off.
4. Sudden or abrupt changes in behavior can be indications of important employee problems.
5. Problems should be dealt with as soon as possible after they are identified.
6. The attitude of the supervisor may have more to do with solving problems than the techniques of problem solving.
7. Correction of employee behavior should be resorted to only after the supervisor is sure that training or counseling will not be helpful.

8. Be sure to document your disciplinary actions.
9. Make sure that you are disciplining on the basis of facts rather than personal feelings.
10. Take each disciplinary step in order, being careful not to make snap judgments, or decisions based on impatience.

AA. Five Important Processes of Management
1. Planning
2. Organizing
3. Scheduling
4. Controlling
5. Motivating

BB. When the Supervisor Fails to Plan
1. Supervisor creates impression of not knowing his job
2. May lead to excessive overtime
3. Job runs itself—supervisor lacks control
4. Deadlines and appointments missed
5. Parts of the work go undone
6. Work interrupted by emergencies
7. Sets a bad example
8. Uneven workload creates peaks and valleys
9. Too much time on minor details at expense of more important tasks

CC. Fourteen General Principles of Management
1. Division of work
2. Authority and responsibility
3. Discipline
4. Unity of command
5. Unity of direction
6. Subordination of individual interest to general interest
7. Remuneration of personnel
8. Centralization
9. Scalar chain
10. Order
11. Equity
12. Stability of tenure of personnel
13. Initiative
14. Esprit de corps

DD. Change

Bringing about change is perhaps attempted more often, and yet less well understood, than anything else the supervisor does. How do people generally react to change? (People tend to resist change that is imposed upon them by other individuals or circumstances.

Change is characteristic of every situation. It is a part of every real endeavor where the efforts of people are concerned.

1. Why do people resist change?
   People may resist change because of:
   a. Fear of the unknown
   b. Implied criticism
   c. Unpleasant experiences in the past
   d. Fear of loss of status
   e. Threat to the ego
   f. Fear of loss of economic stability

2. How can we best overcome the resistance to change?
   In initiating change, take these steps:
   a. Get ready to sell
   b. Identify sources of help
   c. Anticipate objections
   d. Sell benefits
   e. Listen in depth
   f. Follow up

II. Brief Topical Summaries

   A. Who/What is the Supervisor?
   1. The supervisor is often called the "highest level employee and the lowest level manager."
   2. A supervisor is a member of both management and the work group. He acts as a bridge between the two.
   3. Most problems in supervision are in the area of human relations, or people problems.
   4. Employees expect: Respect, opportunity to learn and to advance, and a sense of belonging, and so forth.
   5. Supervisors are responsible for directing people and organizing work. Planning is of paramount importance.
   6. A position description is a set of duties and responsibilities inherent to a given position.
   7. It is important to keep the position description up-to-date and to provide each employee with his own copy.

   B. The Sociology of Work
   1. People are alike in many ways; however, each individual is unique.
   2. The supervisor is challenged in getting to know employee differences. Acquiring skills in evaluating individuals is an asset.
   3. Maintaining meaningful working relationships in the organization is of great importance.
   4. The supervisor has an obligation to help individuals to develop to their fullest potential.
   5. Job rotation on a planned basis helps to build versatility and to maintain interest and enthusiasm in work groups.
   6. Cross training (job rotation) provides backup skills.

7. The supervisor can help reduce tension by maintaining a sense of humor, providing guidance to employees, and by making reasonable and timely decisions. Employees respond favorably to working under reasonably predictable circumstances.
8. Change is characteristic of all managerial behavior. The supervisor must adjust to changes in procedures, new methods, technological changes, and to a number of new and sometimes challenging situations.
9. To overcome the natural tendency for people to resist change, the supervisor should become more skillful in initiating change.

C. Principles and Practices of Supervision
1. Employees should be required to answer to only one superior.
2. A supervisor can effectively direct only a limited number of employees, depending upon the complexity, variety, and proximity of the jobs involved.
3. The organizational chart presents the organization in graphic form. It reflects lines of authority and responsibility as well as interrelationships of units within the organization.
4. Distribution of work can be improved through an analysis using the "Work Distribution Chart."
5. The "Work Distribution Chart" reflects the division of work within a unit in understandable form.
6. When related tasks are given to an employee, he has a better chance of increasing his skills through training.
7. The individual who is given the responsibility for tasks must also be given the appropriate authority to insure adequate results.
8. The supervisor should delegate repetitive, routine work. Preparation of recurring reports, maintaining leave and attendance records are some examples.
9. Good discipline is essential to good task performance. Discipline is reflected in the actions of employees on the job in the absence of supervision.
10. Disciplinary action may have to be taken when the positive aspects of discipline have failed. Reprimand, warning, and suspension are examples of disciplinary action.
11. If a situation calls for a reprimand, be sure it is deserved and remember it is to be done in private.

D. Dynamic Leadership
1. A style is a personal method or manner of exerting influence.
2. Authoritarian leaders often see themselves as the source of power and authority.
3. The democratic leader often perceives the group as the source of authority and power.
4. Supervisors tend to do better when using the pattern of leadership that is most natural for them.
5. Social scientists suggest that the effective supervisor use the leadership style that best fits the problem or circumstances involved.
6. All four styles—telling, selling, consulting, joining—have their place. Using one does not preclude using the other at another time.

7. The theory X point of view assumes that the average person dislikes work, will avoid it whenever possible, and must be coerced to achieve organizational objectives.
8. The theory Y point of view assumes that the average person considers work to be a natural as play, and, when the individual is committed, he requires little supervision or direction to accomplish desired objectives.
9. The leader's basic assumptions concerning human behavior and human nature affect his actions, decisions, and other managerial practices.
10. Dissatisfaction among employees is often present, but difficult to isolate. The supervisor should seek to weaken dissatisfaction by keeping promises, being sincere and considerate, keeping employees informed, and so forth.
11. Constructive suggestions should be encouraged during the natural progress of the work.

E. Processes for Solving Problems
1. People find their daily tasks more meaningful and satisfying when they can improve them.
2. The causes of problems, or the key factors, are often hidden in the background. Ability to solve problems often involves the ability to isolate them from their backgrounds. There is some substance to the cliché that some persons "can't see the forest for the trees."
3. New procedures are often developed from old ones. Problems should be broken down into manageable parts. New ideas can be adapted from old one.
4. People think differently in problem-solving situations. Using a logical, patterned approach is often useful. One approach found to be useful includes these steps:
   a. Define the problem
   b. Establish objectives
   c. Get the facts
   d. Weigh and decide
   e. Take action
   f. Evaluate action

F. Training for Results
1. Participants respond best when they feel training is important to them.
2. The supervisor has responsibility for the training and development of those who report to him.
3. When training is delegated to others, great care must be exercised to insure the trainer has knowledge, aptitude, and interest for his work as a trainer.
4. Training (learning) of some type goes on continually. The most successful supervisor makes certain the learning contributes in a productive manner to operational goals.
5. New employees are particularly susceptible to training. Older employees facing new job situations require specific training, as well as having need for development and growth opportunities.
6. Training needs require continuous monitoring.
7. The training officer of an agency is a professional with a responsibility to assist supervisors in solving training problems.

8. Many of the self-development steps important to the supervisor's own growth are equally important to the development of peers and subordinates. Knowledge of these is important when the supervisor consults with others on development and growth opportunities.

G. Health, Safety, and Accident Prevention
1. Management-minded supervisors take appropriate measures to assist employees in maintaining health and in assuring safe practices in the work environment.
2. Effective safety training and practices help to avoid injury and accidents.
3. Safety should be a management goal. All infractions of safety which are observed should be corrected without exception.
4. Employees' safety attitude, training and instruction, provision of safe tools and equipment, supervision, and leadership are considered highly important factors which contribute to safety and which can be influenced directly by supervisors.
5. When accidents do occur, they should be investigated promptly for very important reasons, including the fact that information which is gained can be used to prevent accidents in the future.

H. Equal Employment Opportunity
1. The supervisor should endeavor to treat all employees fairly, without regard to religion, race, sex, or national origin.
2. Groups tend to reflect the attitude of the leader. Prejudice can be detected even in very subtle form. Supervisors must strive to create a feeling of mutual respect and confidence in every employee.
3. Complete utilization of all human resources is a national goal. Equitable consideration should be accorded women in the work force, minority-group members, the physically and mentally handicapped, and the older employee. The important question is: "Who can do the job?"
4. Training opportunities, recognition for performance, overtime assignments, promotional opportunities, and all other personnel actions are to be handled on an equitable basis.

I. Improving Communications
1. Communications is achieving understanding between the sender and the receiver of a message. It also means sharing information—the creation of understanding.
2. Communication is basic to all human activity. Words are means of conveying meanings; however, real meanings are in people.
3. There are very practical differences in the effectiveness of one-way, impersonal, and two-way communications. Words spoken face-to-face are better understood. Telephone conversations are effective, but lack the rapport of person-to-person exchanges. The whole person communicates.
4. Cooperation and communication in an organization go hand in hand. When there is a mutual respect between people, spelling out rules and procedures for communicating is unnecessary.
5. There are several barriers to effective communications. These include failure to listen with respect and understanding, lack of skill in feedback, and misinterpreting the meanings of words used by the speaker. It is also common

practice to listen to what we want to hear, and tune out things we do not want to hear.
6. Communication is management's chief problem. The supervisor should accept the challenge to communicate more effectively and to improve interagency and intra-agency communications.
7. The supervisor may often plan for and conduct meetings. The planning phase is critical and may determine the success or the failure of a meeting.
8. Speaking before groups usually requires extra effort. Stage fright may never disappear completely, but it can be controlled.

J. Self-Development
1. Every employee is responsible for his own self-development.
2. Toastmaster and toastmistress clubs offer opportunities to improve skills in oral communications.
3. Planning for one's own self-development is of vital importance. Supervisors know their own strengths and limitations better than anyone else.
4. Many opportunities are open to aid the supervisor in his developmental efforts, including job assignments; training opportunities, both governmental and non-governmental—to include universities and professional conferences and seminars.
5. Programmed instruction offers a means of studying at one's own rate.
6. Where difficulties may arise from a supervisor's being away from his work for training, he may participate in televised home study or correspondence courses to meet his self-development needs.

K. Teaching and Training
1. The Teaching Process
Teaching is encouraging and guiding the learning activities of students toward established goals. In most cases this process consists of five steps: preparation, presentation, summarization, evaluation, and application.

   a. Preparation
   Preparation is two-fold in nature; that of the supervisor and the employee. Preparation by the supervisor is absolutely essential to success. He must know what, when, where, how, and whom he will teach. Some of the factors that should be considered are:
   1) The objectives
   2) The materials needed
   3) The methods to be used
   4) Employee participation
   5) Employee interest
   6) Training aids
   7) Evaluation
   8) Summarization

   Employee preparation consists in preparing the employee to receive the material. Probably the most important single factor in the preparation of the employee is arousing and maintaining his interest. He must know the objectives of the training, why he is there, how the material can be used, and its importance to him.

b. Presentation
In presentation, have a carefully designed plan and follow it. The plan should be accurate and complete, yet flexible enough to meet situations as they arise. The method of presentation will be determined by the particular situation and objectives.

c. Summary
A summary should be made at the end of every training unit and program. In addition, there may be internal summaries depending on the nature of the material being taught. The important thing is that the trainee must always be able to understand how each part of the new material relates to the whole.

d. Application
The supervisor must arrange work so the employee will be given a chance to apply new knowledge or skills while the material is still clear in his mind and interest is high. The trainee does not really know whether he has learned the material until he has been given a chance to apply it. If the material is not applied, it loses most of its value.

e. Evaluation
The purpose of all training is to promote learning. To determine whether the training has been a success or failure, the supervisor must evaluate this learning.
In the broadest sense, evaluation includes all the devices, methods, skills, and techniques used by the supervisor to keep himself and the employees informed as to their progress toward the objectives they are pursuing. The extent to which the employee has mastered the knowledge, skills, and abilities, or changed his attitudes, as determined by the program objectives, is the extent to which instruction has succeeded or failed.
Evaluation should not be confined to the end of the lesson, day, or program but should be used continuously. We shall note later the way this relates to the rest of the teaching process.

2. Teaching Methods
A teaching method is a pattern of identifiable student and instructor activity used in presenting training material.
All supervisors are faced with the problem of deciding which method should be used at a given time.

a. Lecture
The lecture is direct oral presentation of material by the supervisor. The present trend is to place less emphasis on the trainer's activity and more on that of the trainee.

b. Discussion
Teaching by discussion or conference involves using questions and other techniques to arouse interest and focus attention upon certain areas, and by doing so creating a learning situation. This can be one of the most

valuable methods because it gives the employees an opportunity to express their ideas and pool their knowledge.

c. Demonstration
The demonstration is used to teach how something works or how to do something. It can be used to show a principle or what the results of a series of actions will be. A well-staged demonstration is particularly effective because it shows proper methods of performance in a realistic manner.

d. Performance
Performance is one of the most fundamental of all learning techniques or teaching methods. The trainee may be able to tell how a specific operation should be performed but he cannot be sure he knows how to perform the operation until he has done so.
As with all methods, there are certain advantages and disadvantages to each method.

e. Which Method to Use
Moreover, there are other methods and techniques of teaching. It is difficult to use any method without other methods entering into it. In any learning situation, a combination of methods is usually more effective than any one method alone.

Finally, evaluation must be integrated into the other aspects of the teaching-learning process.

It must be used in the motivation of the trainees; it must be used to assist in developing understanding during the training; and it must be related to employee application of the results of training.

This is distinctly the role of the supervisor.